D1639156

# SOME SAID IT THUNDERED

**By the same author**

*Come Holy Spirit*
*Does God Speak Today?*


**Contributions to:**
Michael Harper
*Bishop's Move*
Kevin Springer (ed.)
*Riding the Third Wave*
(Marshall Pickering)
Jill Dobson and David Lonsdale
*Can Spirituality be Taught?*
(British Council of Churches)

# SOME SAID IT THUNDERED

Meaningful encounters with some present-day prophets in Kansas City and means for evaluating their prophecies

## David Pytches

> Then a voice came
> from heaven . . .
> the crowd said . . .
> it had thundered!
> John 12:28–29

> Some knew they had heard God
> speak and obeyed him. Others
> attributed the sound to a natural
> phenomenon and dismissed it.
> Yet others accepted it was extra-
> ordinary but could not believe
> that it came from God.

HODDER AND STOUGHTON
LONDON   SYDNEY   AUCKLAND   TORONTO

All biblical quotations are taken from the New International Version, unless otherwise stated in the text.


**British Library Cataloguing in Publication Data**
Pytches, David
    Some said it thundered.
    1. Christian life. Religious experiences
    I. Title
    248.2

    ISBN 0-340-52835-4

*Copyright © David Pytches 1990. First published in Great Britain 1990. Second impression 1990. All rights reserved. No part of this publication may be reproduced or transmitted in any form or by any means, electronic or mechanical, including photocopying, recording, or any information storage and retrieval system, without either prior permission in writing from the publisher or a licence permitting restricted copying. In the United Kingdom such licences are issued by the Copyright Licensing Agency, 33-34 Alfred Place, London WC1E 7DP. The right of David Pytches to be identified as the author of this work has been asserted by him in accordance with the Copyright, Designs and Patents Act 1988.*

*Published by Hodder and Stoughton, a division of Hodder and Stoughton Ltd, Mill Road, Dunton Green, Sevenoaks, Kent TN13 2YA. Editorial Office: 47 Bedford Square, London WC1B 3DP.*

*Photoset by Avocet Robinson, Buckingham.*

*Printed in Great Britain by Cox & Wyman Ltd, Reading.*

To Barry Kissell, my dear friend, whom I inherited as a colleague, since he had already been on the staff of St Andrew's Church, Chorleywood for many years. His faithfulness to God and boldness in stepping out for him has evoked my unwavering admiration as he has ministered both at home and abroad in the power of the Holy Spirit; his unique gift for communicating the Word of God in such original and relevant ways has so often refreshed and stimulated my understanding of the Kingdom of God and the Gospel of Jesus Christ; his gentle and creative gift in leading the Body of Christ into the presence of God in worship has enhanced some of the richest spiritual experiences of my life; his humble listening and loving counsel to individual clergy and laity alike has been an example to observe with awe and to model with delight; this, together with our almost daily fellowship in prayer, his outrageous sense of fun, and loyal friendship in the service of Christ, has made our twelve years of working together some of the most memorable and worthwhile in my life. Thanks be to God!

# Contents

# Acknowledgments

I want to express my appreciation to the Kansas City Fellowship for their ready permission for me to quote from their unedited tapes and so on. I must also put into print my very warm thanks to my wife Mary, my daughter Debby and her husband John, along with the following good friends: Brian and Gill Skinner, Richard and Prue Bedwell, Peter and Ann Scott, Teddy and Margaret Saunders and Mike Pilavachi, who have all most patiently checked my manuscript for readability and hopefully my mind for gullibility and sanity! I have been most grateful for their wise comments and kind warnings. I am also deeply indebted to David Wavre of Hodder and Stoughton for his constructive criticism and careful editing. In the end I have had to make my own judgment over the credibility of everything I am sharing within these pages. I have written as matters honestly appear to me. If the substance of what is related here is true, as I sincerely believe it is, then, however unpalatable it may be to some (as prophets and prophecy have ever tended to be), the Church of Jesus Christ needs to know. Something very significant is being confronted here.

David Pytches

# Introduction

At a recent conference (August 1989) held in Denver, Colorado, which was organised for pastors worldwide of the Vineyard Christian Fellowship, Bob Jones, a prophet from Kansas City (not to be confused with the founder of a North American fundamentalist university), approached an afternoon visitor amongst the *conferencistas* and asked him what he was doing there since he was not a pastor. This was not by way of reproach but out of curiosity.

'That's correct! I am not in fact a pastor,' said the intruder 'and I do not pretend to be a pastor, but my son is one and I have come to visit him.'

'Well,' said the prophet, 'it's strange, since you should not really be here, but I saw you in a vision last night. Another strange thing is that you are not a prophet either and yet you have seen the earth from the heavenlies! What is more you have been searching for the remnants of Noah's Ark on Mount Ararat but you have been looking for it in the wrong place. And you are going to find it.'

Bob Jones then described the 'correct' location in some detail as he had 'seen' it in his vision and his words seemed meaningful to the man he was addressing.

'The discovery will be a sign of a spiritual revival breaking out in that region,' added the prophet.

'That's amazing!' replied the intruder.

'I have in fact seen the earth from the heavenlies, since I was an astronaut and I have walked on the moon. My name is James Erwin. Furthermore, for some time now I have been leading a "Flight Foundation Expedition" team each year to the region of Mount Ararat searching for any remains of the Ark!'

Probably the reader will say that he is not impressed by this kind of report because clearly an astronaut who had walked on the moon would be easily recognisable and his pastimes well-known. This 'prophet' had most likely been given the low-down on the astronaut by the organisers of the conference or others present. There could be a number of natural explanations to account for the story. Was it really likely today that God would reveal such information directly to some 'prophet'! Suffice it to say that a number of sane and reasonable people who were at the conference believed that Bob Jones actually had these facts revealed to him by God.

Bob Jones is one of a number of prophets that Christians are becoming increasingly aware of, who are apparently being raised up in the Church. Whatever are we Bible-loving Christians to make of it all? Dismiss it, discuss it or declare it?

This book combines some personal accounts of extraordinary prophecies and some personal encounters with a number of very ordinary prophets with a few potted biographies to set the material in context. The intention has been to show how such prophets and prophecies have already proved productive for the leadership in a local church situation. There seems to be the promise of great blessing through the availability of prophecy to the wider Church.

I am attempting to show in this book how the leadership in one local church has learned to cope constructively and to great advantage with such an unaccustomed and unusual dimension and/or intrusion into its corporate life. It also reflects something of the swing of my personal reactions, from fascination and wonder to the anger of an outraged intellect; the fear of blame for possibly encouraging a plague of phoney prophets or the debasing of true Christian spirituality to a dial-a-prophecy way of life; the threat to ecclesiastical order and the fate of ostracism from other Christian brothers: all this and then back to a gradual acceptance and a positive assessment.

The increase and impact of such 'divine intelligence' through prophecy will prove a great challenge to our sophisticated churchmen and women in these days of spiritual confusion; it will also create a stimulus to holiness of life in the present climate of moral corruption once it becomes widely recognised that God is disclosing the secrets of men's hearts, even to what is being said in the director's boardroom or the king's bedchamber (2 Kgs 6:12). And finally it will be an evangelistic 'sign . . . for unbelievers . . . he will be convinced . . . So he will fall down and worship God, exclaiming, "God is really among you!" ' (1 Cor. 14:22–25).

Please read on!

# 1

# Kansas City Airport and a Flight Back in History

It was Saturday, 6 May 1989. We had just flown into Kansas City following our third series of conferences arranged for us by the Episcopal Renewal Ministries at centres across the USA. Our team included Richard and Prue Bedwell, my wife Mary and myself.

It was getting late on that Saturday evening. The temperature was hot and we were weary. Mike Bickle, the leader of the Kansas City Fellowship, was arranging for someone to meet us, but as yet our suitcases had not appeared on the airline luggage conveyor-belt, and we were not expecting our 'collector' to materialise for a few more minutes.

I spent these waiting moments casually reflecting on how we had come to be here of all places. 'This is crazy!' I thought. 'What we need is a complete rest after those hectic conferences — not to start meeting a whole lot more people!' My mind flitted back to Monday 7 November the previous year when our old friend John Wimber had come for a two-day visit to rest in our home following his recent conference in Edinburgh.

## An extraordinary story
He had asked us if we could also host another North American pastor, a fellow-speaker from that same conference.

'Hi, David,' he drawled in his friendly Californian

accent, as he introduced him, 'Meet my good friend Mike
Bickle. I think you'll find he has an interesting story to
share.'

John had never spoken a truer word! What Mike had
to share with us blew my mind. He told us an extraordinary
story about his experiences with some prophets. He had
originally treated these prophets with very great suspicion
but in the course of double-checking their revelations he
had finally come round to accepting them as being from
God.

Through one of them apparently he had been led to
found a new church in Kansas City. That had been some
six years previously. They now had a regular attendance
of about 1500 at each of their Sunday services at the Grandview Worship Centre, a building originally constructed as
a sports complex. They had already branched out into five
other fellowships across Kansas City (with another 1500
membership between them) and they had a vision for
planting forty-five more such fellowships in Kansas City
within the next ten years.

In these days of Church decline in the West this was very
exciting news indeed and I could not resist asking if it would
be possible for us to visit him and his church the next time
we were in the States. Not only did he seem to welcome
the idea but he offered to provide hospitality for us. He
also said he would try to arrange a meeting with some of
these prophets.

## The first surprise

And now at last we were here in Kansas City and wondering
what on earth we were letting ourselves in for. Suddenly
there was a friendly shout and turning round we saw Mike
Bickle himself coming to meet us. He was accompanied
by two men who were both unknown to us. Our friend
introduced the first as Geoff Grisamore, who was about
twenty-seven years old. He and his newly-wed wife Mary

Ellen had most kindly offered their home to the four of us so that we could all be together for the weekend. Geoff was taking charge of our baggage. Then Mike introduced the other man: a medium-sized, gentle, grey-haired man aged between fifty-five and sixty.

'David,' he said, 'I'd like you to meet Paul Cain.'

We greeted and then as Paul was shaking hands with the others Mike took me to one side and explained that this man was one of the prophets though he did not like being addressed as such, nor did he ever refer to himself in that way.

Introductions over, we took our luggage out to the waiting transport and loaded up. It seemed quite a long haul from the airport to our destination. We stopped about half-way at the place where Paul was going to stay and he got out. I had been sitting beside him in the minibus. He had seemed very relaxed. He had a good sense of humour. He was tired from his travels, as we certainly were.

There being no need to make polite conversation to the by now empty seat beside me I found myself reflecting on prophets in the Christian Church down the ages. In fact I had been doing quite a lot of reading about them before leaving the UK. It would be true to say that I was definitely intrigued but not too kindly disposed towards them. My religious upbringing had conditioned me to be suspicious. Who wants to be 'conned' by a false prophet?

## Prophets of the past

History, I reflected, had not treated the prophets too well, to be sure, from the time of Montanus (*c.* 170) down to our present day. Admittedly we only know about most of them through their critics. All sorts of weird accusations had been laid to their charge, some cynically invented and others sinfully exaggerated. Having said that, however, there were undoubtedly yet other charges which it would have to be admitted were only too true. England had her fill of strange prophets. Those from the time of Oliver Cromwell (1599—1658) were especially remembered. That was supposed to be the age of the Spirit when any believer could receive a word from the Lord and speak it out!

Many freelance prophets (some known popularly as the 'Ranters') were soon up and about. Cromwell even appointed some of these as chaplains to the army. On at least half a dozen occasions between 1647 and 1654 the council meetings of the Protector himself were interrupted by prophets, apparently without protest. But while some of the prophets in circulation at the time may have been genuine there were many others who were obviously not. Sadly but understandably it is the latter who are best remembered!

## Pseudo-messiahs

In London in April 1561 John Moore was whipped and imprisoned for saying he was the Christ. Similar treatment was meted out to his companion William Jeffrey, who claimed to be St Peter. A month later a 'stranger' was set in the stocks for calling himself the 'Lord of Lords and King of Kings'. The following year Eliseus Hall, a draper, was arrested for assuming the title of 'Eli, the Carpenter's Son' and claiming to have had a vision from God following a two-day return visit to heaven and hell.

In 1586 a shoemaker from Essex named John White claimed to be John the Baptist, while Ralph Purden, a minister from the same county, was claiming that he would lead the saints to Jerusalem. The next year Miles Fry alias Emmanuel Plantagenet believed that he was the son of Queen Elizabeth by God the Father and that his authority was greater than the Angel Gabriel's. Usually such self-appointed 'prophets' were dismissed as brain-sick, but the threat to law and order prompted the attention of the authorities.

William Hacket, a discharged soldier and illiterate

bankrupt, persuaded himself (1591) that he was the 'Messiah' who had come to judge the world on God's behalf. He proceeded to travel around London with two disciples, Edmund Copinger and Henry Arthrington — one he appointed a 'prophet' of mercy and the other a 'prophet' of judgment. Between them they publicly challenged the highest authority in the land.

Yet another 'Messiah' was Wightman, an Anabaptist and Arian (today's equivalent of a Jehovah's Witness), who in 1612 became the last Englishman to be burnt at the stake for heresy. He claimed to be the prophet Elijah, foretold in Malachi (4:5), and warned that those who denied his claims would be mauled to death by wild bears just like those young louts who mocked Elijah's successor, Elisha. (2 Kgs 2:24). These threats did not save Wightman from a cruel execution.

## Power to inflict plagues!

The antics of these 'Messiahs' were closely paralleled by the case of the two weavers, Richard Farnham and John Bull, who attracted a good deal of public attention in 1636. They too claimed to be divinely inspired prophets but with this difference: they were armed with powers to inflict plagues upon mankind and the knowledge of all things to come: 'I am one of the Two Witnesses spoken of in the eleventh chapter of Revelation,' declared Farnham. 'The Lord has given me the power for the opening and the shutting of the heavens.' Notwithstanding, both men were locked up in very earthly prisons and died there in 1642. This was not before they had issued promises to their followers that they would rise again and reign for ever.

The claim to be the Two Witnesses of Revelation (ch. 11) was revived later by the tailors John Reeves and Lodwick Muggleton who established a small sect during Cromwell's time, announcing themselves to be the forerunners of Christ endowed with the keys of heaven and hell.

**Enter the women**

The best known of the prophetesses before the Civil War was Lady Eleanor Davis (later Douglas) the daughter of the Earl of Castledown, who was married first to Sir John Davis and then Sir Archibald Douglas. In 1625 she claimed to hear a word, a 'Voice from Heaven' early in the morning, speaking as through a trumpet: 'There is nineteen years and a half to the Judgement Day.' From then until her death in 1652 she was continuously given to such prophetic utterances and spent many spells in prison for her pains.

She was believed to have accurately predicted the deaths of several leading public figures as well as that of her first husband. Her ecstatic and utterly enigmatic pronouncements were frequently printed, and as frequently suppressed. In a commentary she wrote on Daniel in 1633 she made dark predictions about the fate of Archbishop Laud and Charles I. Her commentary was published illegally in Amsterdam, and for this she was fined and imprisoned by the High Commission.

Some years later she went berserk in Lichfield Cathedral, defiling the altar hangings and proclaiming from the bishop's throne that she was the Primate of all England! No one of course could be deceived but she had to be restrained. However she was not without serious supporters including the politician Edward Dering who fully accepted that she had genuine foreknowledge. The refugee Queen of Bohemia and the Anglican divine Peter de Moulin were also her champions.

**Short cut to free speech**

Prophetesses were becoming quite the thing. This may have been partly because within the culture of the times women had no other accepted medium for public expression. The same of course was true for the ordinary working-class man and probably explains why so many of them also adopted the convenient but counterfeit guise of the prophet. A readily available 'word from the Lord' gave the message immediate authentication and was the best guarantee that one's voice would be heard whenever and wherever one wanted.

Jane Hawkins, a Huntingdonshire woman, had visions of the downfall of the bishops of the Church of England in 1629! Grace Carey, a Bristol widow, claimed to be seeing visions as early as 1639 which forewarned of the coming Civil War. She followed the King around urging him to make reforms before it was too late! For this and further fascinating research into the Ranters and so on the reader is referred to Professor Keith Thomas's *Religion and the Decline of Magic* (especially ch. 5 on Prayer and Prophecy).

The Church was hardly prepared for the novelty of such prophets. Some were for believing them; others for banning them. John Owen, a moderate and scholarly Puritan, appointed by Cromwell to be Vice-Chancellor of Christ Church, Oxford, was the first theologian to produce a thorough biblical treatise on the Person and Work of the Holy Spirit. The book, *Pneumatologia*, was an attempt to introduce some godly order on the subject.

## Fifth Monarchy Men

The whole prophetic phenomenon of the Ranters lasted about thirty years and only faded with the fall of the Fifth Monarchy Men. They had supported Cromwell during the time of the Commonwealth. These fanatics believed the time had come for the fulfilment of Daniel's prophecy concerning a fifth and messianic kingdom to follow those of Babylon, Persia, Greece and Rome. When these Fifth Monarchy Men saw their hopes fading they suddenly rose and terrorised London. For this they were quickly put down and with them prophecy also.

## Prophecy and social change

Prophecy had become associated with social revolution. Religious freedom was perceived as having gone too far! The restoration of the monarchy saw the introduction of much restrictive legislation: the Corporation Act, the Quaker Act, the Act of Uniformity and the Five Mile Act. The governing classes were determined to prevent the possibility of any return to the situation that had prevailed during the years of Cromwell's Commonwealth.

But in spite of all the abuses of prophecy down the ages there must have been some good reason why a man of the distinction of Tertullian had thrown in his lot with Montanus; or why the Wittenberg professor Andreas Carlstadt, a co-labourer in the Reformation with Martin Luther and Philip Melanchthon, had supported the prophets of the oppressed peasants in Zwichau – one a local weaver by the name of Claus Storch and the other Luther's former student, Thomas Munzer.

Montanus, 'the mouthpiece of the paraclete', was appealing for purity in a Church which was degenerating through sophistication and formalism; while Munzer was appealing to the Reformation leaders for their open support and protest against the oppression of the peasants, which was prevailing so ruthlessly at that time (1520–). Both, it would seem, were raising issues which needed redress.

## Enthusiasts

Down the centuries there had been many illuminist and millenarian movements inspired by prophetic leaders, each flourishing briefly under the general description of 'Enthusiasts'. These nearly always reflected a yearning for a purer Church and a closer relationship with God. A Jesuit historian has discerned a close similarity between all these movements: 'The hypothesis of a genuine connection is almost irresistible' (Ronald A. Knox, *Enthusiasm*). Could there be something of the Holy Spirit behind this 'connection', we ask?

In his book *The Ante-Nicene Fathers* (1895) F. J. A. Hort selected five main characteristics of such movements, which I have slightly edited. Their similarity with what is happening today is significant:

1 A strong faith in the Holy Spirit as the promised paraclete present as a heavenly power in the Church of the day.
2 A belief that the Holy Spirit was manifesting himself supernaturally through entranced prophets and prophetesses.
3 An inculcation of a specially stern and exacting standard of Christian morality and discipline in the teachings of these prophets.
4 A tendency to set up prophets against bishops. (The Montanists saw real spiritual danger in the apparently accommodating role of the episcopate to the powers of the State.)
5 An eager anticipation of the Lord's second coming as imminent and a consequent indifference to ordinary human affairs.

## Lack of policy for developing prophecy

The Church has yet to develop a constructive policy for regulating prophetic activity within her ranks — a need first frankly recognised in the *Didache* (written some time between the first and the third century), which dealt with the problem too crudely to be helpful. A policy was still needed for dealing with prophecy without quenching the Spirit (1 Thess. 5:19) to encourage its development appropriately. However, no generally acceptable way had yet been advocated, probably because prophets have never been generally acceptable! (2 Chron. 18:7b; Hos. 9:7b). Their messages (even when genuine) have too often proved disagreeable (Jer. 15:10), especially to people who have itching ears only for what they themselves want to hear (2 Tim. 4:3), rather than what the Spirit is saying to the churches (Rev. 3:22).

## Rule of thumb approach

The simple and spontaneous rule of thumb reaction through the centuries seems to have been to vilify and persecute the prophets themselves — an age-old practice which the Lord himself thoroughly condemned. This nihilist approach has dominated the perceptions of the Church throughout history. How often have we been reminded of the good Bishop Butler's famous words to John Wesley after their meeting in 1739 when he said: 'Pretending to extraordinary revelations from the Holy Ghost is a horrid thing, a very horrid thing!'

There are no records available of direct contributions from the Montanists and Anabaptists themselves to help the modern-day researcher. We do not even know if Montanus or the later Anabaptists ever committed their own prophecies or views to paper (though we know there are some prophecies attributed to individuals among them). Therefore mainly negative impressions remain on spontaneous subliminal recall to snuff out any hint of on-going supernatural revelation for the Church of today.

'The chief effect of Montanism on the Catholic Church was greatly to reinforce the conviction that revelation had come to an end with the apostolic age, and so to foster the creation of a closed canon of the New Testament,' wrote Henry Chadwick (*The Early Church*, p. 15). Thereafter most believers assumed that the completion of the New Testament was the limit of God's revelation and to all practical purposes taught that God would never speak again apart from and through the Bible. The idea of a modern-day prophet who believed he had received revelations directly from God for himself, another individual or the Church, would be a matter of ridicule in most ecclesiastical quarters today.

## Was the age of revelation over?

Professor Chadwick names Irenaeus as 'the last writer who can still think of himself as belonging to the eschatological age of miracle and revelation'. Born about AD 125 Irenaeus was Bishop of Lyons from AD 177–202. It is instructive to read what Irenaeus himself wrote since his life and ministry are supposed to have rounded off a defined period of Church history. We may find his actual words on the subject in his work, *Against Heresies*, where he says:

> For which cause also His true disciples, having received grace from Him, use it in His name for the benefit of the rest of mankind, even as each has received the gifts from Him. For some certainly do drive out demons so that those who have been cleansed from evil spirits frequently both believe and join themselves to the church. (Book I)
>
> Others have *foreknowledge of things to be, and visions and prophetic speech* [italics mine], and others cure the sick by the laying on of hands and make them whole. Yea, moreover, as I have said, the dead even have been raised up and remained among us for many years. And what shall I say more? It is not possible to name the number of gifts which the Church throughout the world has received from God in the name of Jesus Christ. (Book V; Eusebius, *Ecclesiastical History*, ch. vii, AD 316.)

It was not that Irenaeus had any problems about accepting a canon of Scripture then in the process of being recognised; indeed he was one of the first defenders of the concept. He recognised the real value of a 'canon' or fixed list of authoritative writings of approved orthodoxy, especially in his fight against heresy. But it is plain that Irenaeus, like both Tertullian and Montanus, was convinced that the living God was still speaking to the Church through revelations of the Holy Spirit according to his promises contained within the New Testament canon.

**Early Church prophets**

After his ascension the victorious Christ endowed the
Church and 'gave . . . some to be prophets' — an office
which was distinct from that of the evangelist, pastor,
teacher or apostle, who were all to prepare God's people
for works of service so that the Body of Christ might be
built up (Eph. 4:11—12). He also sent his Holy Spirit at
Pentecost and through the Spirit the nine 'spiritual gifts'
spelt out in 1 Corinthians 12:7—11 were manifested in the
New Testament Church. One of these (which is to be eagerly
desired [1 Cor. 14:1—3]), was the gift of prophecy (v. 12:10).
Later in the same chapter Paul explains how (in the Church)
God has appointed prophets (v. 28), among others. Then,
through his questions at the end of Chapter 12, Paul shows
clearly that not all are prophets — but by the same token
prophets would have been there somewhere!

**A present-day prophet**

Paul Cain would certainly fall into the category of a present-
day prophet. Unlike the other prophets that Mike Bickle had
mentioned, Paul did not live in Kansas City but came from
Dallas. It was there that he had received revelations from
the Lord which had been forwarded by telephone to John
Wimber in Los Angeles (though the two had never actually
met) via a third party. This was during the time of a
leadership crisis in the Vineyard Christian Fellowship at
Anaheim, which John Wimber had founded ten years
earlier. He had been astounded at the insight of Paul Cain
who had provided him with such very perceptive
information, which Paul could not possibly have gained
from any human source. In spite of his doubts about the
availability of such a high level of revelation from God to
the Church today the precision of this message persuaded
John to take Paul's very wise advice seriously — and wise
indeed it proved to be, as events at Anaheim turned out.

Realising that this must be the very man John Wimber

had described to us back in the UK, we felt pleased now that we had been able to meet Paul Cain, and even more delighted to learn that he was booked by Mike Bickle to preach on the following evening at the Kansas City Fellowship worship centre where we had planned to be. It was going to be an interesting weekend.

## 2

# Little Brother — the Boy Prophet

We were very much looking forward to hearing Paul Cain preach on the Sunday evening and arrived to find the church already packed. It was clear that his ministry was well known and highly respected in Kansas City. Before Paul preached a lady gave a remarkable testimony.

She described a one-off visit she had received from Paul Cain, whom she had never met before, while she was a long-term patient in a mental institution in California some years earlier. Her story of miraculous restoration to health followed by her discharge within a matter of days served admirably to raise the level of faith of the congregation. Paul was then given the microphone to address us.

## Our disappointment

It is difficult for me to say what I thought. I had to admit I was disappointed. His style was reminiscent of some of the Pentecostal preachers I had heard during my time of missionary service in Chile, but I was cross with myself for feeling antagonistic over his presentation. There were amazing swings in his style that certainly made one listen attentively.

Flights of sheer oratory and profound scriptural insight poured forth, followed by solemn calls to repentance, righteousness and holiness of life. One felt that heaven was about to descend and both the glory and the judgment of God would burst upon us at any moment.

On the other hand he was certainly no expository or orderly preacher. Intermittently he would crack some corny quip, alternating with frequent apologies for being confused, then groaning over an apparent physical affliction that was troubling him — the kind of drawing attention to oneself that makes the average Englishman cringe slightly. We had heard that he suffered from a weak heart and feared a collapse was imminent.

## Was it our fault?

Now that I think I understand these things a little better I suspect the confusion and pain that was inflicted upon him originated from our direction. We had been introduced to him as good friends but were feeling pretty uptight with our many criticisms and disappointments. Some of the negative energy from this was probably disturbing his sensitive soul. We had no idea at that stage that he could pick up such 'vibes'.

We learned later that at another conference, where there were over 3000 in attendance, that he had become aware of the presence of three hostile people somewhere in the crowd. They were spies from a certain seminary in another state and had come in looking for data to destroy his reputation. He knew their names by revelation from God. He knew where they had come from and what their criticisms were without ever having met them. He mentioned that he was aware of their presence and motives in the course of his address but did not publicly identify them and the men in question did not reveal themselves.

Someone else present told him afterwards that he had recognised the people concerned who were personally known to him. When Paul Cain then named them, the friend corrected him over the first name of one of them; but it turned out that Paul was right — it was simply that the man was not commonly known by his first name, which was the one that had been revealed to Paul.

**Affront to rationality**

Our overall problem seemed to be the sheer effrontery of
Paul's approach to our rational minds. In the end he closed
apologetically, seeming suddenly to give up. There had been
no clearly anointed ministry to conclude, as had obviously
been anticipated by many of the congregation including
ourselves. We went home to chew it all over. 'Whatever was
all that about?' we wondered!

We were beginning to hear the strangest of stories
concerning Paul Cain. My curiosity was getting the better
of me and I was determined to find out why this gentle and
humble man with the silver hair and the sometimes golden
tongue was held in such high esteem by these people.

Mike Bickle had warned us to beware if we wanted to get
to the real truth. When it came to encounters with God, Paul
was a master of the understatement and tended to down-
play everything. Paul does not want to be referred to as a
prophet − he does not like anything which might tempt him
to think more highly than any Christian ought to think of
himself. He especially abhors anything that hints of
superstardom in the Church. His master and model is Jesus
Christ who made himself of no reputation.

This is one of the dangers of writing a book like this:
people might try to put Paul Cain on a pedestal. That would
be counter-productive to the message Paul is bringing to the
Church − that the day of the superstars is over; that God
will not share the glory that belongs to him and that he is
looking for humility. He sees that God is deliberately
operating today through a new breed of workers −
ordinary, dedicated lay people. Paul wants everyone to know
that he too is simply an ordinary, earthen vessel and nothing
more. Mike Bickle, who knows Paul well, says that when
Paul indicates that the Lord wants him to say or do
something it usually follows one of his frequent angelic
visitations.

## A miracle baby

His fascinating story began in 1929, one of the most turbulent years in recent US history, when Paul was still in the womb of Anna Cain, his forty-five-year-old mother. His Jewish father, William Henry Cain, fifty-six and poor, eked out a living as an odd-job man. His mother was sick with heart problems, besides being 'terminally' ill with TB. She also had cancerous tumours in her uterus and breasts. She was taken from her home in Garland, a small farming community about twenty miles from Dallas in Texas, to the university hospital at Dallas. A St Louis physician, renowned for cancer research and treatment, used her as a test case for a new cancer treatment. When he pronounced her incurable she was discharged and returned to Garland to die.

Once home among the cotton fields and the birch spinneys she took her cause to Jesus. She had a strong faith in the Lord. Like Hannah (in 1 Sam. 1:10–11), she promised to dedicate her offspring to the Lord. She cried out to him until, at the hour past midnight (ever a sacred hour to her from that day to this), the Lord appeared in the form of an angel. Touching her on the shoulder with his right hand he made her a wonderful promise: 'Daughter, be of good cheer, you shall live and not die. The fruit of your womb is a male child whom I shall anoint to preach my gospel like the Apostle Paul; and you shall name him Paul.'

Her healing was immediate. Specialists reported it as the first time in medical history that new tissue had been restored to diseased breasts. When the time came she gave birth to a baby boy, just as the Lord had said, and of course she called his name Paul. He was nursed at the very breasts which had so recently been riddled with cancer. Her doctor called her a miracle woman. She is now, at the time of writing, in her 105th year!

## God called him by name

Anna Cain never talked to Paul about the Lord's call upon his life until the Lord himself had revealed this directly to him when he was eight years old. As a child Paul was misunderstood by other children because he did not enjoy the same things as they did. He was nicknamed 'Droopy Eyes' and was terribly shy. Even then he was aware of a supernatural power which guided many of his actions and as early as he could remember he wanted to be a preacher. Paul had already had a conversion experience at the age of seven, which gave him, to use his own words, an insatiable love for Jesus. He soon found himself taking long walks through the cotton fields with Jesus.

One evening as he was worshipping in his local Baptist church he became especially conscious of the Lord's presence upon him. This feeling stayed with him all the way home and when he reached the house he had a sense that somehow God was going to speak to him. Suddenly he heard the Lord call his name! In utter terror he rushed for cover under the bedclothes.

Thinking she might be protecting him his fourteen-year-old sister Mildred asked the Lord to speak to her instead! But the Lord had an audible message for the boy under the bedclothes. His sister heard it all and has ever since been a committed lifetime supporter of Paul's ministry. Paul Cain has never shared with anyone all the sacred burden of that message except to say that if he kept himself pure the Lord promised him a ministry which would reach the masses — that he would preach the gospel through healing.

Having heard his mother recount the miracle of her own healing, without which he could never have been born, combined with his personal commission from the Lord to heal, it is not surprising that Paul Cain has never had a problem in believing in divine healing. Paul's mother, grandmother and great-grandmother had all been born with the gift of 'seeing'. His great-grandmother would sometimes see things in broad daylight and ask if anyone else could see them too. If they said they could not she would then lay her hand upon them and they would immediately see the identical vision. This seems very similar, in effect, to Elisha's prayer for his servant (2 Kgs 6:17) when he prayed that the Lord would open the servant's eyes to see what Elisha saw — and he did.

Paul now found he was 'seeing' also and would know things that were going to happen to classmates at school or were happening to absent friends. He knew simple things like who would end up with a bloody nose or who would win a race, and the other children recognised that what Paul said came true. Paul, the eight-year-old, had also become an avid reader of the New Testament. His class teacher was very understanding and when he was in the fourth grade she appointed him 'chaplain' and he would read the Bible and preach to his class! He was of course regarded as abnormal amongst his peers. He found this difficult to come to terms with for a long time. He resented being different and found himself beginning to withdraw from people. He jokes about it now: 'For years I resented being abnormal but when I found out what being normal was I wanted to be abnormal again!'

## Preaching to spikes

Knowing he was going to be an evangelist Paul used to go out into the fields to preach. He would collect disused railway spikes, the large-headed kind used for pinning rails to wooden sleepers. He would arrange these spikes in rows like people sitting in pews. His childhood dream of a big congregation was easily satisfied. He would simply go out and collect more spikes to increase the attendance at his meetings. Then he would preach to them over and over again. He said there was never any response — they were too hard-headed — but at least they could not get away!

Paul claims to have built his first 'church' by the time

he was nine years old! He used fencing boards for the walls and his aunt gave him some whitewash to paint them. But the place badly needed a roof. There was an outhouse in their back yard which Paul did not think was being put to much good use at the time and which had a roof. It was a nicely shingled roof just like any proper church would have. Paul, with the help of some of his classmates, moved it from the outhouse to cover his church. Before his new church could ever be dedicated, however, he was to receive the biggest whipping of his life from his father. Mr Cain insisted that the roof was needed right where it had come from!

By this time his Baptist pastor had also discovered that Paul was seeing and hearing things which others apparently could not see and hear. He could see when a person was going to be healed and live and also knew when someone was going to die. This made him feel very uncomfortable. Despite Paul's tender years, the Rev. Dr Paris began to take him out with him on his pastoral visits. Paul would know — perhaps by how people were dressed in his visions — which ones the Lord was going to heal and when they prayed for them healing would often come immediately. One incident Paul recalls from those early days was the case of Mary. Long before they reached the hospital he described to his pastor that in one ward they would meet a lady of about sixty robed in a rose-coloured housecoat. She would be in bed dying with cancer and at the foot of the bed would be her brother Thomas, standing dressed in his working clothes. When they arrived at the ward they saw the scene exactly as Paul had described it and when they prayed for Mary she was immediately healed, just as Paul had predicted. Dr Paris would encourage Paul to keep his eyes on God's call to be a preacher, though this was hardly necessary in the circumstances.

## Paul's public ministry

By the age of nine 'Little Brother' (as he was being

affectionately referred to by adults, perhaps because it was the form of address used by the angel who so frequently spoke to him) began public preaching in a limited way. He had gathered a 'big' crowd of about ten or twelve neighbourhood kids, besides his grandmother and his parents, and they sang and praised God at his meetings. Public preaching for a boy of that age was something, not surprisingly, which the Baptists found hard to handle. Increasingly Paul was being invited to evangelistic healing meetings run by Pentecostals. Their leaders seemed to have fewer problems about a boy prophet, as they called him, having seen the anointing of the Lord upon him.

About 500 people attended Paul's first big preaching meeting in Dallas. When he stood up in front he became so frightened that he started shaking and could not speak! The people believed that such fearful shaking was a sign of the Holy Spirit's presence upon him (though Paul Cain imagined it was sheer fright), and they began to rush forward confessing their sins and getting saved and healed. The young Paul stood watching in amazed silence as he continued shaking for about thirty minutes before he sat down. The next day the news spread that revival was breaking out at the young preacher's meetings!

By the time Paul was fourteen he had a regular radio ministry and was conducting healing services in a small tent. He began travelling across America ministering as an evangelist and healer. Those were the early days of the healing movement which swept through the Pentecostal churches during the forties and fifties under the leadership of men like William Branham, Oral Roberts, T. L. Osborn, A. A. Allen, Jack Coe and some ten other names well known in those days.

Though he could not really understand why, Paul began to find himself resented and even rejected by some of the leaders (not necessarily any of those named above), possibly because they felt his youthfulness tended to bring discredit on the healing movement; possibly because he still had much to learn of the Christian graces and had not yet matured into that model of spiritual discretion and sensitive diplomacy which is so much the mark of the Paul Cain one meets today. But then again, possibly, though Paul does not say so, the resentment was present because of the extraordinary anointing that was upon him, and there was not a little jealousy.

### William Branham's story

However, one man who encouraged him greatly was the late William Branham, now regarded as the pioneer of the post-war healing revival. There were strong similarities in their 'anointings', an often-used word which calls for an explanation. In my own particular Christian tradition we hardly ever use the word in the sense intended here. This kind of 'anointing' is the clear manifestation of the working of the Holy Spirit in a person through revelations, prophecy and supernatural signs.

Such an anointing was certainly upon William Branham. He was born in 1909. His parents were poor and his home was a dirt-floor log-cabin built among the Kentucky hills. Although he was apparently the child of non-Christian parents an extraordinary light appeared in the room where he lay newborn. This did not last long, but long enough to be the talking-piece of his hill-billy neighbourhood for many years to come.

Then, when he was aged three, he received a divine visitation that was followed by another when he was seven. He was making his way back from the well to his home when his attention was attracted by loud rustling in a leafy poplar tree beside the path. He looked up and saw what appeared to be the effect of a mighty wind in the tree but then noticed that other trees nearby were not touched by it. Curious, the little boy stood still, peering at it more intently. Suddenly he heard the awesome roar of a voice and recognised his own name. The young William was terrified and rushed home as fast as his legs would carry him. Once there he hid himself under the bedclothes never moving till the following morning.

Some years later, after experiencing a personal healing, Branham received the call to preach through an angel and became an independent Baptist pastor. His ministry was blessed by a revival in Jeffersonville, Indiana, where he later built a large tabernacle.

Branham did not actually hear that voice again for thirty years; then one day he happened to be in a cave, and the voice sounded forth once more, the same voice he had heard when he was seven. As a result of this visitation in 1946 Branham was given power to discern people's illnesses and the secrets of their hearts.

## Legend of spiritual power
In his *All Things are Possible: the healing and charismatic revivals in modern America* (1975), D. E. Harrell Jr says that 'The power of a Branham service . . . remains a legend unparalleled in the history of the charismatic movement.' This assessment is further attested in *The Pentecostals* (1977) by Walter J. Hollenweger, who once acted as Branham's interpreter in Zurich. Hollenweger wrote that he was 'not aware of any case in which he (Branham) was mistaken in the often detailed statements that he made'. These details concerned the people who were about to be healed.

When Branham conducted his packed healing meetings, orderly queues would form up beside him and he would preach in between ministering to the sick. Sometimes he would seem to be searching for something to say; if one was unaware of his way of ministering it was helpful to hear him remind the people that he could not pray for their healing until the angel of the Lord had appeared to him. He would say to the public, 'You all know what I am waiting for. I can't do anything until he comes.' Once he had the assurance of the angel's presence Branham would turn to the person and tell him details concerning himself and also the nature of his complaint, all of which apparently was being revealed to him supernaturally. He would then lay hands on the person quickly and tell him to go his way — he was healed! Invariably this would prove to be the case.

Branham died in 1965, having taken his prophetic preaching and ministry of healing and deliverance to the far corners of the earth right to the end of his life.

Recently my wife and I were fortunate enough to see some early TV recordings of Branham and his public ministry, and were pleasantly surprised by the self-effacing character of this humble but extraordinary man of God — so very much in contrast to many (though certainly not all) of the latter-day, image-minded TV evangelists in the USA. By all accounts William Branham lived moderately and dressed modestly. There was no suggestion of showmanship in those films that we saw.

## A special bond

There was always a special bond between William Branham and Little Brother through their healing ministries. They frequently ministered and evangelised together in the early days, and whenever Branham could not meet a commitment he would send Cain in his place.

The extent of their spiritual 'sight' was phenomenal. When they called each other by phone one would often say to the other in fun, 'You're all right today. How am I?' and each would know the other's state of health precisely.

On one occasion after Mike Bickle had been complaining to his wife that he had 'a bit of a sniffle' — a slight cold — something he rarely had, the phone rang. Bickle picked up the receiver and heard Paul on the line. He had heard about Paul's gift so he said by way of a joke, 'Hi, Paul! You're all right today! How am I?' Immediately Paul answered him, 'Why, Mike, you've got a bit of a sniffle and you are all wet. Your hair is standing up on the left side of your head.'

Bickle called his wife Diane to look at him. 'Sweetheart, Paul says I have a "sniffle", I am all wet and my hair is standing up on one side. Am I all wet?'

'Yes,' she said. 'You've just come out of the shower!'

'And is my hair standing up on one side?'

'Yes,' she replied, 'on the left side!'

Paul Cain calls these strange experiences 'little tokens' that the line is still open with the Lord.

## Some unorthodox teachings

It is important for the record to say that though Dr Hollenweger was not aware of any case where Branham 'was mistaken in the often detailed statements that he made', he was undoubtedly referring to the revelations which Branham received about situations, circumstances and people he was ministering to, and not to all his doctrinal statements. Here it seems that in his later years Branham may have fallen into serious error.

Due partly to ignorance arising from his lack of any theological training, and isolation arising out of his style of revelatory leadership, corrective theological insights were not easily available to him. Neither could he have been immune to the inevitable temptations concerning his own 'superior' knowledge and ministry, which may have blinded his judgment in some areas.

Whether he was actually at fault or not, history is clear that Branham's unique record became tarnished with some unbiblical teachings that have been attributed to him — though his supporters claim they were the work of others who exploited his good name; such as his last administrator who founded a sect called the Branhamites after his death. These have been further distorted by later detractors. In any case no man is infallible, however effective or remarkable.

Paul Cain claims personally to have been unaware of false teaching in Branham but that could have been because he rarely ministered with Branham latterly, but only in his place. Whatever the case may be, Paul has openly and completely dissociated himself from any of the strange teaching attributed to Branham either during or after his lifetime. He does remember Branham being seriously worried over some of his 'followers' who referred to him as 'Elijah'. He had mentioned this to Paul, presumably over the telephone, and remarked that if they persisted in that sort of thing the Lord would remove him. He died shortly after that very comment.

None of this can alter the impact of an amazing healing ministry to the glory of God; nor to the evangelistic impact of his simple and direct words about Jesus and the cross.

# 3

## Disillusionment with Superstardom

When still a teenager Cain went to Tulsa, Oklahoma, certain he was led by God, to call on the Rev. Dr Ward. The latter (later to become a firm friend and fellow-speaker at conferences with Paul) was the pastor of the famous Bethel Temple (Assemblies of God), which at the time was suffering a serious decline in the size of its congregation. Paul Cain brought some personal 'revelations' concerning the pastor and an offer to conduct a healing campaign to help him build up the church in Tulsa.

Obviously stunned by the accuracy of the revelation which had clearly come from the Lord, Dr Ward replied, 'Little Brother, I believe God has sent you and I will discuss it with our elders at their board meeting tonight.' The next day when Paul returned to learn of their decision he heard that the answer was 'No'. The elders clearly did not want a 'little child' to lead them.

### The working of the gift

So he went to Raymond T. Richie, who at one time had had a remarkable healing ministry but was now in the same town pastoring the independent Revival Temple (with a much larger seating capacity than Bethel Temple) where there was another congregation also declining in numbers. Cain explained what had happened at Bethel Temple and offered his services to Richie, who was more than convinced by yet more revelations about himself which Paul proceeded to

share with him from the Lord. He arranged for Paul to begin
the next Sunday.

It was during this campaign that Paul, for the first time,
experienced in public the working of the 'gift', as he called
it. He was looking at a man in the meeting and found
himself saying, 'Sir! I perceive you have the faith to be
healed' — and so he was. He then caught sight of a lady
in a polka-dot dress and gasped out in surprise, 'Oh, Sister!
You in the polka-dot dress — you come from San
Antonio!' 'Yes,' she answered. (Paul was silently amazed
to have been shown this accurate fragment of information.)
He looked at her again and saw an amber light upon her.
He called out, 'Oh Sister! Get up out of that chair!' At
this she shot up, kicking over a couple of crutches in the
process, and began to run round the aisles completely
healed and praising God.

A mighty movement of God was soon being launched
which was to reach several thousand people. Dr Ward of
Bethel Temple attended those meetings, both praising God
each time he witnessed the working of God's miraculous
power and wringing his hands with sadness each time he
recollected that God had originally intended to bless Bethel
Temple in that way and it had been his own elders who had
closed the door to it.

## Reading the instructions

Nowadays Paul teaches very carefully that it is essential to
'read the instructions' which come with the gift and not to
get carried away as he had in those early days. He tells some
embarrassing stories against himself to make the point. Very
soon Paul was calling people out in public and telling them
the secrets of their hearts. Not surprisingly things began to
get rough for him at that stage. Dr Richie took him on one
side and said, 'Little Brother, your gifting is wonderful. You
are called to heal the sick but you've been pointing out the
sins of some of my best members!' Paul did not realise it

then but his days in Tulsa were definitely numbered.

He had yet to understand about 'the instructions' — the kind of thing that Jesus was talking about when he said to his disciples, 'I have much more to say to you, more than you can now bear' (John 16:12). Earlier Jesus had said to them: 'The Father who sent me commanded me what to say and how to say it' (John 12:49). Words of knowledge sometimes need to be used with words of wisdom.

## Move to Sacramento

Dr Richie quietly arranged for Paul to transfer to Sacramento and continue his healing ministry in California where he said their need was greater! The good pastor omitted any mention of the revelation of secrets when he commended Paul to his pastor friend in Sacramento. The first meeting there was held in the Governor's Hall.

Once again incredible things began to happen, as Paul Cain recalls: 'I almost ruined my meeting. I jumped to my feet and pointed out one of the ushers — a real bruiser standing at the back. "You old hypocrite," the Lord says, "How can you stand there and have anything to do with what's going on at this meeting when you know what's going on in your own heart. You are planning to go off with that lady over there [he was pointing directly at her] at the end of this week and to leave your wife over there [and he pointed now at the wife — both the wife and the other woman were totally unknown to Paul but he identified them through the Spirit]. She has your three children and you are deserting them. You old hypocrite!" ' The accused man began striding down the aisle towards Paul while the other ushers tried to dissuade him. 'Leave him alone: he can't touch the man of God!' said Paul, who shudders now to recall how very grandly and smugly he pronounced those words. The next thing was that the usher had dropped his collecting bag and was running towards the platform. He was within a yard of Paul when he was suddenly struck down to the floor. Looking up sobbing, he cried out, 'It's all true — what must I do?'

Paul then caught sight of another lady and pointing at her he said: 'And you lady, if you don't repent I'm going to tell everyone what you've been doing in room no. 202 in your motel today.' The lady in question fell to the floor crying out in repentance. And there was a lot more of the same to follow. Paul continued 'naming people — and who was messing with whom.' The power of God descended that night. When it came to the end the pastor of the church was nowhere to be seen. Paul had to dismiss the meeting himself.

## The pastor's early phone call

The next morning he had an early phone call. It was a simple message relayed to him in his hotel saying that the pastor wanted him to listen to his radio broadcast just coming on the air. Paul Cain tuned in. 'Folks!' it was the pastor's voice, 'we are in the midst of a great revival. Last night something happened that I have never seen before. The preacher called the people out. He told them their sins, who they were committing them with, and where they were committing them. Someone said to me afterwards, "Where were you, Pastor?" "Well," I admitted, "I was under the grand piano confessing all my sins!" ' So now the news was all over town.

When the pastor met Paul later he said, 'Young man, we must protect ourselves. If this keeps going someone's going to drop down dead like Ananias and Sapphira' (Acts 5). Perceiving biblical precedent the young and ever innocent Paul replied, 'Oh, that would be wonderful. Let's pray it will happen!' 'Are you crazy?' replied the pastor. 'They'd put us in prison.' His heart leaping once again at the glorious prospect of sharing the fate of the early disciples, Paul responded, 'Oh, I want that to happen too!' The pastor shook his head uncomprehendingly and turned away muttering to himself, 'We'll have to do something.' That night when Paul drew near to the meeting place he saw a huge banner had been suspended outside the front of the hall, which read: THIS IS A PENTECOSTAL REVIVAL and underneath was written: ENTER AT YOUR OWN RISK!

There was another large church in California where Paul was invited to preach whose pastor was in the process of building a mega-church. During the meetings, however, every time Paul sensed the anointing of God's Spirit upon him, a particular lady in the congregation would interrupt him with some ecstatic utterance. Paul bore it patiently a couple of times, as his New Testament namesake had put up with the slave girl's interruptions in Acts 16, but after the third and then the fourth time he rebuked her publicly. When she did it yet again Paul warned her: 'All right sister, if you do that once more I will expose you!' Paul returned to his theme again and was no sooner off in full rhetorical flight when she interrupted yet again. This time Paul said: 'Lady, don't do that. You are an unclean vessel. You must not minister in these gatherings. You are living in adultery', and he included further details to convince her that this was no guess.

The pastor of the church closed the meeting forthwith and announced that the rest of the week's programme for which Paul was billed to speak was cancelled. This had never happened to Paul before and he asked the pastor why he had done it. 'Because you have lost your burden for souls,' came the reply.

Sensing that he needed to double-check that the pastor really meant what he had said (since Paul heard the Lord telling him it was a lie), Paul asked him point blank: 'Is that the real reason? Are you sure of that?' 'Yes,' replied the pastor, 'that is the only reason.' 'Oh!' said Paul, 'I wish you had not said that because the real reason is that that lady is married to a millionaire in your congregation who is giving you three million dollars to build your new church. That is why you are closing down my ministry here.' 'That's

a lie,' snapped the pastor angrily. 'Oh!' said Paul, beginning
to weep, 'I just wish you had not said that as the Lord has
told me that now you will never live to preach in that new
church building.'

Then it was the pastor's turn to weep. He begged Paul
to take back that awful word. 'If you withdraw I will invite
you back to my new church often and you can have some
great ministry there,' he said. As Paul was telling the story
he said that it gave him no satisfaction at all to say this but
the day the new church was finally opened the pastor was
in the vestry before the service when he collapsed of a heart
attack from which he never recovered.

Wherever Paul was invited God's blessing was clearly
evident. He found that by spending all the day in prayer
God would give him picture after picture of people and their
illnesses and many other particulars about them, such as
where they would be seated and how they would be dressed
and so on. Paul saw cancers shrivel and fall off and the dead
raised. While he was still only eighteen, his biography had
been published telling story after story of the power of God
to heal and to save. Paul shudders today at the very idea
of a book on his life when he had seen so very little of it,
but worse still he deplores the possibility of readers
attributing any glory to him when it must all belong to the
Lord!

**First public humiliation**
Paul discovered that other healing evangelists did not spend
nearly as much time in prayer as he did and neither did they
fast but would go out to meals with friends while engaged
on their missions. Paul's custom was to spend several hours
a day shut up with the Lord waiting for his message and
seeking to 'know' who the Lord wanted to minister to in
particular. His desire for the presence of the Lord was so
intense that he would sometimes ask his helpers to lock him

into his cell where he could be alone with the Lord all day. He would blindfold himself on the way to the services so that he could not see anything to distract him from the visions the Lord had so clearly given him.

One day he convinced himself that he really need not take this thing so seriously and that it must be a gift that he had been born with. He decided that he should behave a little more sociably, like other evangelists when they conducted their meetings. He went to his tent service as usual and the Lord showed him a lady who was in need of prayer. He began by describing her symptoms and was about to tell her her name, as he had done so often in the past, when his mind went completely blank. 'Oh!' he cried out, 'I have sinned before the Lord. The anointing has lifted from me. I cannot pray for any more tonight. I must go back to my room and repent.' He left thousands of people behind him in the middle of the meeting and could not return until the following evening when it was all sorted out with the Lord again.

Paul Cain was one of the first healing evangelists to go on television. In 1952 he began to film his miracle services and these were shown weekly on secular TV stations. A businessman had fallen in love with Paul's ministry and bought him what had been the world's largest tent in those days. It would seat 8000 people and was soon extended to seat 12,000. (He had bought it from another healing evangelist named Jack Coe who was having an even bigger tent made for his meetings.)

On one occasion Paul found himself greatly troubled by a lady who followed him round from meeting to meeting and took it upon herself to tell him each time he preached how stupid and ridiculous he was. He was really perplexed to know how to deal with this. After prayer he felt he should preach a sermon on the sins of the tongue. He made an appeal at the end of it suggesting that people might want to come forward and put their tongues (he meant it in a symbolic way) on the altar. Once again up came the lady, who assumed Paul had meant it literally and began once more to criticise him. 'How ridiculous! How could I put my tongue on that altar?' she snorted sarcastically. Paul's quick wit got the better of him and before he could resist it he heard himself saying, 'Well, ma'am, why don't you put on as much as you can and let the rest hang over?'

## Call to walk alone
Paul used to go to a retreat place called 'A Thousand Oaks' on Lake Sherwood near Santa Maria in California, that belonged to a friend. This was a wonderful, quiet place where he could go to prepare himself for his meetings when he was speaking in the area. He was driving back there from San Francisco one night after a meeting, thinking of his engagement to marry a girl he had fallen in love with, when the Lord suddenly appeared beside him in the front seat of the car dressed in a monk's black habit and wearing a skull cap! He told Paul he was jealous of this particular friendship: 'If you really want the kind of intimate walk with me you profess to want you must remember that I walked alone,' he said. That was not the whole substance of the conversation which seemed to last quite a little time, but was the part Paul has felt free to share of this supernatural encounter.

Suddenly Paul became conscious of lights flashing behind him. There was certainly nothing supernatural about them! He braked as the highway patrolman flagging him down was stopping in front of him. The latter was trembling as he came back to Paul and shone his torch all round the interior of the Lincoln he was driving.

'Where is he?' demanded the cop in a shaky voice.

'Where's who?'

'Where is the man that was sitting in the front seat talking with you?'

'Oh!' said Paul in his southern drawl. 'That was the Lord.'

'Wow!' said the patrolman glancing strangely at Paul and then sighting his Bible on the dashboard. 'Are you a minister?'

'Well yes, you could say that,' Paul responded.

'Then do you realise that you and the Lord have just gone through three red lights together?' He was not joking. He was breathing heavily. 'I really don't know what to do about this,' he continued, thinking about his duty as a highway patrolman. 'Listen, if you and the Lord will go and book up for the night in that motel up the road we'll forget the whole affair!' He muttered to himself. 'Oh Lord! How much I would like to forget this!' Once again he looked strangely at Paul and then let him go.

'Aren't you going to give me a ticket?' said Paul.

'Oh, no!' said the cop. 'How could I ever give the Lord a ticket?'

Did the patrolman really accept Paul's explanation? Paul said later that he must have been a Catholic cop! Who else would have believed him?

As he drew nearer to the lake where the retreat house was the Lord reappeared. Although he was fairly used to this kind of surprise by now it was always awesome. After the Lord had finished discussing some other matters with him Paul felt it was a good opportunity to raise the question of his recent engagement to be married. So he told the Lord about it and asked: 'What do you think of it, Lord?'

The Lord just looked at him kindly.

'But what do you really think about it? You don't seem very pleased. Don't you want me to be married?'

The Lord looked at him again and repeated softly, 'I walked alone.'

'Lord,' said Paul, 'if you don't want me to be married I am willing to give up the idea but you will have to do something about my feelings.'

The Lord replied by simply placing his hand upon him. To Paul it felt as though fire passed right through his body.

From that day to this, he says, he has never experienced any further sexual desire. That was Paul's initiation into celibacy.

Walking alone has had other problems, however. A prophet is frequently rejected and needs encouragement. When Paul refers to the 'cruel essence of loneliness' it is clear he knows what he is talking about. It is something he has had to endure for long years. In an address he lamented our sick society that assumes that everyone who had chosen or been called to celibacy by the Lord is judged by the world to be 'gay' and even suspected of it by other Christians. 'There seems to be no place,' he says, 'for a Protestant celibate. Catholics understand it and are much more accepting.'

## Renouncing fortunes

His calling to a single lifestyle was further tested when his friend, a former president of the National Bankers' Life Insurance, died. He was one of the richest men in the world and had provided Paul with his 12,000-seater tent. In his will he left his entire fortune to Paul with one condition only, that Paul got married. There was a particular lady Paul's benefactor had in mind, apparently. Paul renounced the fortune.

And that was not the only time that Paul had to do such a thing. On another occasion he ministered healing to Mary Virginia, a prominent member of the famous Hutton family, who had broken her back in an accident. When she died some years later she left her personal fortune to him along with that of her lately deceased brother. But the Lord told Paul not to take a dollar of it or he would lose his anointing. This was the second fortune that Paul renounced.

On yet another occasion a wealthy Californian judge who had made a fortune out of oil asked Paul to stay at his bedside as he died. The man was horribly demonised and death was a most frightening ordeal for him. Paul agreed to visit him and the judge left Paul $8 million – not such a large fortune as the others but more than enough for Paul. It was well known that the judge had hired a sorcerer to find the oil which made him so rich and the Lord told Paul not to touch the money on pain of death. Telling these stories years later Paul says he had never had occasion to regret the Lord's restrictions upon him.

In 1956 Paul began planning to publish a magazine for an extensive readership. This would also serve to promote his work and the making of more films like *The Beginning of the End*, which he had made in 1954 and had proved so successful – even for church-planting in South America.

## Call to Europe

News of the great blessings on Paul's ministry was being noised abroad and wherever he held meetings great crowds showed up. Besides a tent for the congregation, and a prayer tent, Paul had a tent for invalids with often over 1000 stretcher and wheelchair cases brought in for healing. Hundreds would be miraculously healed. On one particular day, when Paul was ministering with Jack Coe, they prayed for over 2000 individual cases. People walked out of their wheelchairs, were healed of their cancers, received their sight and were delivered of demons. There were healings of all kinds. Paul also worked with Demos Shakarian, the founder of the Full Gospel Business Men's Fellowship. Often during the night Paul would see visions of the people God was going to heal the next day. On one occasion he 'saw' a couple steal into hospital and kidnap their own child, a crippled polio victim, to bring to the meeting. The Lord showed him where they would be sitting in the tent the next day; and as had so often been the case before, when he got to the tent he saw them there just as he had seen them in the vision. Paul singled out the couple, and described to them how they had 'kidnapped' their own child from hospital to bring to the meeting; before their very eyes the crippled leg was straightened out to match the other through the power of the Lord.

He tells the story of how on one occasion he wanted to buy a car. A salesman took Paul for a drive and asked him what kind of a minister he was. When Paul said that he was a Christian minister the salesman shrugged. 'I hope you are not like those healers on TV,' he said. By way of reply Paul simply repeated a conversation the salesman had very recently had with his wife in private. The man paled and became very serious. 'You probably already know this then, but the transmission is out on this car. In fact none of the cars in this lot is any good. Don't buy any of them!'

By 1957 Paul was beginning to sense strongly that the Lord was going to call him to minister in Europe and was concerned about how the fares would be paid. He had never travelled abroad before. He was booked to minister in Washington and had decided (without apparently seeking the Lord about it) that he would ask for the offering at the biggest meeting and put that aside for his travel expenses to Europe.

Without knowing anything about this, his mother came to him and told him she did not think he should take that offering. He was a little peeved over that because he thought his mother would not know about his call to Europe and how the expenses for this were weighing on his mind. But since this appeared to have been supernaturally revealed to her from the Lord he decided not to take the offering.

Shortly after, he had a call from William Branham telling him that he had been booked to go round Europe ministering but could not now meet the commitment. (In fact Branham had actually sensed the Lord telling him not to go but to send Paul in his place.)

'Would you, Little Brother, go in my place?'

Paul felt very honoured but enquired anxiously, 'What shall I do about the money? I don't have any!'

'Don't worry about that, Little Brother, you won't need

any money. All your expenses will be paid for and I am sending you the ticket.'

Paul was taken to Switzerland, then to Germany. The meetings at Karlsruhe were sponsored by the Lutheran Church and were attended by more than 30,000 a night during one week. At one of those services more than 1500 people received Christ.

# 4

# The Almost Silent Years

Sadly, such invitations from William Branham caused jealousy among older men in the healing ministry, which brought out strong feelings of rejection in Paul. The envy surprised, shocked and sickened the tender spirit of the young evangelist. A kind of rat-race had built up around this ministry. He felt the Lord saying to him he was not to be swept into it. 'Remember if you win that race you are still only a rat!'

Too many of his fellow healing-evangelists were pushing too hard for visibility. This is one of the hazards of independent ministries which need a lot of money simply to keep them on the road (like some of the American televangelism of today). Money and fame were beginning to take their toll. When individual ministries of this kind were threatened there could be a lot of very unchristian back-biting. Paul was beginning to discover what it was like to be the victim of that kind of thing and confesses that he also became critical of those who criticised him.

## A new breed
Some evangelists were even falling into immorality. The Lord spoke to him very clearly one night and told him to get out of that rat-race. He said, 'I am going to take you aside into the desert until a new breed of men is raised up. In the days to come this ministry will be taken forward without superstars.'

He then gave Paul a token promise telling him that his mother would not die till he had stood before this new breed of leaders – men and women who have learned the lessons of the past and will become an army (Joel's army, he called them); who would not love the world, 'the cravings of sinful man, the lust of his eyes and the boasting of what he has and does' (1 John 2:16) – what the Kansas City prophets call the three Gs, 'the girls, the gold and the glory!' They will have learned the lesson and will not bring the ministry into disrepute by falling prey to any of these common temptations.

Paul had become increasingly concerned about the direction his own ministry was taking him. The young boy who had heard the audible voice of the Lord was forgetting the wise counsel that his mother had given him: 'Son, be as little as you can be and let God be as big as he can be.' The personal nature of his ministry which he had once enjoyed so much had vanished. The hundreds of letters he was receiving from needy people had to be attended to by others. Paul had no time even to read most of them let alone pray for those who sent them. A standard form had been prepared by way of a reply. Paul Cain says he had become so 'big' and was in such demand and drove himself so hard that he had no time to spend with the Lord as he had been so careful to ensure in earlier days.

The crowds were there; the finances were there; glamour and prestige were there; but the voice he had once heard so clearly had grown dull. The telephone was ringing day and night with calls from all over the nation. They all wanted to talk to the 'healer'. They all wanted Paul's prayers and revelations from God about their situation or condition. His phone had to be taken out and Paul had to make himself scarce. He was 'too important' to take phone calls – too busy to make personal visits to pray for the dying.

**Lean times**

Paul was aware that all was not well with his soul. He had lost that intimate relationship he had once so much delighted in with the Lord. But how could he get off the band-wagon while travelling at such speed? One day when plans were being made to publish an even greater magazine which would serve more than ever to get the name of Paul Cain before the people and to keep the finances going for his ministry, a crisis suddenly arose. He was stricken with a near-fatal disease putting his whole ministry in financial jeopardy, causing him to lose all the station-wagons, trucks, cars and equipment that went with his travelling tent ministry. Soon his television programme was taken off the air and the magazine planned for expansion simply folded up.

The months of agony and pain were however a blessing in disguise. He learned what it was to be lonely again and what it felt like to be told by the doctors that his illness was terminal. He must be prepared to die. He also learned fresh lessons of the Lord's mercy and goodness. The Lord had taken him into the desert of loneliness to give him the opportunity of examining his life and ministry and restoring that intimate fellowship he had once so much enjoyed with the Lord. He felt a new longing to get back into that early habit of soaking himself in the Word of God and a ministry that exalted Christ rather than man. He so much wanted to return to that simple walk of faith, being led step by step by the Spirit of God to meet the Lord's appointments. He needed to make the ministry of love his highest priority. 'If I have a faith,' wrote his great namesake — words he knew so well, 'that can move mountains, but have not love, I am nothing' (1 Cor. 13:2). Then he remembered what the Lord had so often said to him: 'Paul, I never called you to be famous; I called you to be obedient.'

Like Evan Roberts of Welsh Revival fame who simply disappeared from the scene (*c*. 1907), Paul renounced everything and went back to his mother's home in Dallas.

He destroyed his collection of newspaper cuttings which reported so many of the signs and wonders he had witnessed. Away went all the testimonies of conversion and healing which he had been involved in during the brief years of his public ministry. Now his still youthful heart yearned for holiness because he knew that that was what the Lord was yearning for him. Paul Cain had to learn holiness the hard way, just as everyone who seeks to be holy does. A little girl once prayed with simple insight and feeling: 'Lord make the bad people good and the good people nice.' She had got something there. Not everyone found Paul's holy life easy to take.

## The Jesus People

In the 1970s California saw a remarkable ministry among the hippies which became known as the Jesus People Movement. Paul was invited to help and was eager to assist in whatever way he could. He was asked to pick up a musical group of recently converted hippies who would be participating in the meeting where he was to speak. He packed them into his mobile home — a sacred vehicle with every part of it prayed over by Paul and dedicated to the Lord. The vehicle was undefiled by drink, smoking, drugs, sexual impurity or foul language of any kind. Paul was horrified to find these Christian hippies drinking, smoking, and possibly taking drugs, while appearing totally insensitive to other people's feelings or possessions. They dropped half-empty beer cans on the floor and their stubbed-out cigarettes littered the interior; they dropped half-eaten food on the carpet and one of them even scratched the glove-box in striking a match. Paul was inwardly furious and would gladly have murdered one of them, but he knew he had to forgive.

Eventually they reached the meeting-place where the Jesus People were to play their part with Paul. As the meeting was drawing to its close Paul sensed the Lord saying that

when the crowd regathered the next day they would witness
the incredible healing of a brain-damaged cripple. Paul was
just about to say this when one of the team gave out an
identical invitation! And so it was! The cripple's name was
Brian and he was miraculously healed, even going up on the
stage to play a musical instrument to prove it. The miracle
was incredible indeed but what was more incredible to Paul
was that the Lord should have used such uncouth youths
to do this. It softened his heart and grace was given for a
great reconciliation between them all. The young men
confessed to him that they had found his 'holiness'
obnoxious but then they apologised for going too far in their
reaction to it. It was another lesson that Paul had the grace
to learn.

## Unnecessary overkill

Sometimes, these days, Paul thinks there may have been a
little unnecessary overkill in his earnest pursuit after holiness.
He regrets some of his hastiness in destroying all those
archives. Perhaps in his old age they would have revived
treasured memories for him of the power and glory of God.
But God knew his motives — those of a rare species of
Christian — unusual especially in one so much and so early
in the public eye. Paul thirsted with holy zeal after
righteousness — no sacrifice or discipline was too much.
He readily embraced the wilderness life for nearly thirty
years.

Paul published an article in the late 1950s describing his
reflections on his own experiences of the healing ministry
and the way the Lord had led him since. This article was
carried by nearly every religious periodical of the day. He
received some 5000 letters about it, and it was republished
several times. Many of Paul's contemporary healing-
evangelists considered this a betrayal and reacted unkindly
to him. But the article proved to be the knife which severed
Paul completely from the past and set him free to walk in

humility and obedience until God was ready to use him again.

Recently God has been reminding him that he has not forgotten the call which is still upon his life. Paul Cain believes that God has shown him that in the last days there is to be a restoration of revelatory prophecy to the Church. He sees this as sharing the visions and messages that God has given him with accompanying signs to inspire a new order of prophets. These would spur on the Church to follow after holiness. They will not dare to touch the glory that belongs to the Lord and they will encourage the faithful to create new wineskins for the revival which is imminent.

## 'End times' outpourings

He quotes Joel's prophecy to which Peter likens the manifestation of the Spirit at Pentecost. The Prophecy of Joel still awaits the complete fulfilment promised for the last days when:

> I will pour out my Spirit on all people. Your sons and daughters will prophesy, your old men will dream dreams, your young men will see visions. Even on my servants, both men and women, I will pour out my Spirit in those days. I will show wonders in the heavens and on the earth, blood and fire and billows of smoke. The sun will be turned to darkness and the moon to blood before the coming of the great and dreadful day of the Lord. (2:28–31)

Paul gives a kind of mini-model of this in his public meetings. Having foretold what God intends to do for and through an individual person, the Church or the nation, Paul will then give a token sign; he will call out someone, usually until that moment completely unknown to him, and then reveal details about that person, some well-known and some that only the individual concerned, or a very limited number of people, could possibly know. Frequently he will identify some ailment — diabetes, cancer, a heart condition, a goitre or some such thing — and speak healing in Jesus' name.

## A sign we checked out ourselves

An acquaintance of ours named Debbie, who works in the Vineyard Christian Fellowship at Anaheim in California and whom we and some of our church members have known for several years, had been married for nearly a decade and all that time she had been wanting and praying for a baby. In spite of all the medical attention and the prayer she had been unable to conceive. She was in Kansas City a short while ago when Paul Cain was ministering at the Olathe Worship Centre, one of the five new centres which have grown out of the original Kansas City Fellowship.

Though neither had met the other before, he identified her by name in a public meeting as someone who was praying for a baby but could not conceive. He told her that God had heard her prayers and that she would conceive that very week. When I met her later she told me she had conceived that very week and was by then several months pregnant. For her this was a veritable miracle. It was also a sign that Paul's prophecy should be taken seriously.

## Power surges

Mike Bickle told me of a particular night that week when Paul had been prophesying and the power of God came down mightily. Everyone began to sense the 'manifest presence of God' powerfully in the room. Mike was speechless. A spirit of great boldness came upon Paul and he reeled off about seven names in rapid succession with accompanying words of knowledge, all of which were incredibly accurate. There were so many spontaneous healings and miracles and so much revelatory information, during sixty to ninety intense, power-packed seconds, that after it everyone just needed to sit in amazement giving glory to God. Silent awe hung over the room.

Suddenly there was the sound of sirens as two fire engines screeched to a standstill right outside the centre. The doors burst open and a number of uniformed firemen with hoses and axes demanded where the fire was. Mike shook his head, hardly able to cope with such an abrupt and earthly 'landing'.

'There is no fire here,' he said.

'Oh, yes, there's a big one somewhere! Down at the station all the signals possible are going for this place. The circuits have blown and set off the alarm system. There are signs of a tremendous power surge,' said the leading fireman, hardly waiting in his frenzied rush to find the fire.

They hunted high and low, of course, as their professionalism dictated. No fire could they find anywhere! Not even a whiff of smoke! And no one in the packed building had panicked. The firemen left completely mystified.

After the meeting Paul turned quietly to Mike and apologised. 'I am so sorry about the fire scare. I should have warned you that that does sometimes happen when there is a lot of divine power about!'

On his first visit to Anaheim in February 1988 Paul saw powerful lights across the room and a strong sense of the presence of God was accompanied by revelations in the word of knowledge. On that occasion an expensive video camera was short-circuited. This was battery-operated and not plugged into any outlet. The next night the telephone system was blown out though no one was on the phone at the time.

Paul Cain has been more or less a recluse in his home for the past twenty-seven years except for the times he has been sent to warn a religious or political leader of something God had revealed to him — as apparently he was sent to warn Jimmy Swaggart (the televangelist) some seven or eight years before his public fall from grace. Other exceptions have been occasionally when he sensed the Lord's leading to speak in a church or at a conference somewhere, where people were ready to experience a Pentecostal visitation once more. Instead of 200 to 250 engagements a year Paul would now go out no more than five or six times and only then on guarantee that there would be none of the kind of promotion or publicity which had attended his earlier ministry.

## Restoration of prophetic office

A couple of years ago Paul received a word from the Lord that he was to visit every evangelical leader of significance in the USA and some beyond. He took a message from the Lord to each of them. He found the responses varied — some listened and some rejected his words. Paul had been charged to find the leader of God's appointing who would give him a public platform to use for the restoration of the prophetic ministry to the Church of Jesus Christ.

Like Samuel with Jesse's sons, after each meeting he had to enquire if there was not yet one more. He had visited about twenty-five Christian leaders in all. He was beginning to run out of all such prominent men that he could think of. But though he felt his health was a continuing problem which limited him seriously he never gave up the search.

# 5

## New Church in Kansas City

As the reader is aware, we first met Paul Cain through Mike
Bickle. It was he who first shared with us both the great
blessing of having a prophet of the Lord in the local church
and a constructive approach to the raising of a prophetic
ministry. This latter will be developed in more detail later
(ch. 11).

### A young leader
Mike Bickle was the leader of the thriving Kansas City
Fellowship but he seemed very young to be heading such
a large gifted team — about twenty-five church-planters,
prophets, teachers, pastors and administrators. Besides his
responsibilities as leader, preacher and teacher, the major
part of his time, like that of the New Testament apostles,
was given over to prayer and study of the Bible. He was
married in 1977 to Diane (née Marion) and has two sons,
Luke, aged eleven, and Paul, nine. His father, Robert
Bickle, had been a world champion amateur boxer
(welterweight) in the 1950s. Mike had grown up in the
champion's home in Kansas City where he had been
educated initially, and then had gone to Washington to study
medicine.

As far as his church background goes he had once been
a Catholic and later a Presbyterian. In his late teens he had
had a personal experience of conversion to Christ. That was
in 1971.

A school friend, David Parker, now on the staff of KCF, still remembers the impact of Mike's conversion on his fellow-students. Mike, like his father who had doubtless contributed to his training as an athlete, was well-built and fully committed to a number of athletic programmes. At the school there seemed to be some kind of a divide between the committed athletes and the leather-jacketed layabout 'greasers'. Every now and then the latter would seek to provoke a fight between the groups if they knew they were beyond the eagle eye of the school authorities. The first time this happened after Mike's conversion, the athletes looked to him for their cue. He would normally have responded to the challenge with considerable gusto. But Mike seemed to have something else in mind. The leader of the greasers took a step forward and held up his fist to him menacingly. 'No!' said Mike, 'I won't fight you because Jesus Christ has told me to love you!' Once again the greaser shook his fist. 'No!' Mike repeated without moving, whereupon the greaser landed him a punch in the face. Mike still did nothing but looked straight at him. It was a tense moment because the athletes knew it was in Mike's power to trounce him at that game. When it was obvious that Mike was not going to respond in kind the leader landed him another. 'No' said Mike, 'I won't strike you − I love you for Christ's sake.' It was too much for the layabouts. They quickly dispersed and their leader, seeing he was almost isolated, strutted away in assumed disgust to hide his shame. It was a telling act of Christian witness. The marks and bruises on Mike's face healed but the impact on his classmates lasted a long time.

Today his five sisters and their husbands all worship at the Kansas City Fellowship, as does Pat, his younger brother, who is paraplegic. Soon after his commitment to Christ, Mike developed a great passion for the Bible. His vast knowledge of the Word of God is widely commented on by all who know him. A mutual friend said he thought it could be the result of Bickle's long-practised habit of turning the Scriptures back into prayer to God.

## A call to full-time ministry

This knowledge and love of the Bible was so marked that he was invited to leave university at twenty and minister full-time to a small group of Bible-loving Christians in St Louis, Missouri. A partner in his ministry there was his friend Bob Scott who continues to work alongside him today as the administrator of the Kansas City Fellowship.

While still at university his father had visited him and talked over the problem of his brother Pat. In 1973, as a teenager, Pat had suffered a broken neck playing American football at High School. Being the son of a father made famous through sport the story of the tragedy had been front-page news in the Kansas City press. In a radio interview following the accident Pat had bravely shared his faith saying: 'God will deliver me one day!' For the family there was now the question of who was going to have the long-term responsibility of looking after Pat in his paralysed condition.

Mike's father had come specifically to ask Mike to promise he would take on that responsibility should anything happen to him. It is not clear whether Mike had any inklings at that time of his father's terminal heart condition, but his father died soon after. At least he had died with one consolation: the assurance he had so badly wanted from his eldest son regarding the future care of Pat.

Since the beginning Pat has believed that God would heal him one day. The heavy responsibility for Pat so willingly taken up was one of the factors which had led Mike to develop his marked discipline for intercession. This in turn has become a distinctive characteristic of the Kansas City Fellowship. There are three two-hour sessions for intercessory prayer there every day.

Mike had been away from Kansas City for just seven years

when he was led back in June 1982 through remarkable circumstances. While still pastoring a church with a membership of over 400 in St Louis, Missouri, he had his first encounter with a prophet whose name was Agustine Alcala.

### An unknown prophet

Agustine was driving past a church one day (it happened to be the one under Mike's leadership but of that Agustine knew absolutely nothing), when the Lord suddenly gave him a powerful prophecy for the pastor there. Since he did not know who this was, Agustine drove to a friend in town and enquired who the pastor of that particular church would be. Did his friend know the man? Yes, indeed he did! The friend told him the pastor was a gifted young man named Mike Bickle.

Agustine then explained that he had a message from the Lord for Mike and would like to speak to him urgently, so this friend called him up on the telephone. 'Hello Mike, I have got a prophet here who has a word straight from the Lord for you. Will you speak with him?' A prophet was really the last thing Mike felt like talking to at that moment. 'That's all I need,' said Mike to himself, 'a prophet!' Frantic thoughts of how to handle such a strange phenomenon were racing through his mind. However should he answer this one, he wondered? Politely and as definitely as he could muster he replied, 'I appreciate your call but thanks — not just now!' and put down the receiver. Mike's later comment was, 'He didn't tell me it was an audible voice he had heard from God — but then I would not have believed him anyway!'

### The prophet goes to church

Agustine then decided he would have to visit the church and see the man himself so he went there and took a seat in the front row. He happened to choose one of those Sundays when for a number of reasons Mike arrived late and slipped quietly into the sound-control booth at the back, unseen by the congregation facing the front. The service was being led by another brother somewhat older than Mike. Some 300 to 400 people were engaged in worship there that morning.

Suddenly Agustine summoned the courage to stand up and introduce himself (something Mike would never allow to happen in his church today). He began, 'Hello! I'm Agustine – the Lord uses me to speak prophetically.' And prophetically he spoke without more ado! At the back Mike was thinking, 'Oh my, those are pretty bold statements!' But Mike was intrigued by it all, not least because he recognised the truth of what the stranger was saying. 'Perhaps someone has been telling him things about us,' thought Mike who just could not make it out. He was viewing it all with caution: 'Maybe yes and maybe no,' he mused.

Then the prophet began to call out three or four people Mike knew well and was telling them things which he realised the prophet just could not have known naturally. He was beginning to admit to himself that he was impressed. Suddenly the prophet turned about to address Mike directly where he was still sitting above the congregation level in the sound-control booth at the back.

### Riddle of the pastor's identity

The prophet, of course, had no idea that the man he was pointing at was the pastor. In fact he was still quite foxed about that because he assumed the older man up front was the pastor – and yet he had been told by his friend that the pastor was a young man! And neither the man up front nor Mike at the back was wearing anything which could distinguish them as ministers – so it really was very confusing for Agustine.

'That young man at the back of the room!'

'Me?' asked Mike.

'Yes you,' said the prophet pointing directly at him.

By this time Mike was totally embarrassed. Everyone, of course, knew who he was except the prophet, who continued, 'Young man, the Lord has called you into the ministry and he is going to redirect your path into something completely new.'

When he had finished a handful clapped and others muttered protests *sotto voce*: Whoever did this man think that he was? And didn't he know that he was speaking to their pastor? How dare he address him publicly as 'That young man!'

Someone asked Mike later if his spirit had witnessed in any way to the prophecy. Mike replied that he had been so confused that he would have to listen to the tape-recorded service afterwards to find out what it was all about!

At the end of the service the prophet made his way towards Mike still not knowing who he was. 'Hey, why don't you come out to lunch with me so that I can get to know you?' he said. 'The Lord has certainly got some powerful things in store for you to do. I'm trying to get to the pastor so that I can invite him out too.'

Mike agreed and when the prophet had found the older man he thought was the pastor they set off together. It was not till they reached the restaurant that it dawned on Agustine who the pastor he was looking for really was!

## A message he did not want

That was more or less how Mike and Agustine first crossed paths personally. But Mike was not about to be taken in; besides he had been very happy in St Louis and was not wanting to leave at all. He had no idea what he was meant to do now about the strange message Agustine was pressing on him.

'I heard the audible voice of the Lord,' insisted Agustine. 'This is a very serious word from God!'

Mike played at being vague: first he did not know what

to think about audible voices! Secondly he did not know what to think about prophecies! And thirdly he did not know anything about this kind of thing at all!

'It's all so completely new to me!' he replied, trying to get the message across that he was not a person to be easily duped.

A week later Mike was visiting relatives in Kansas City, planning on staying there for a few days. This was after he had mooted with the elders in St Louis that they would have to weigh up the prophecy together sometime when he got back. Talking to a minister friend at the Presbyterian church, he and his wife were suddenly asked, right out of the blue, how long they thought they would be staying at St Louis. Mike's wife Diane replied for herself, saying, 'For the rest of our lives! What do you think, Mike?'

'I can never see us leaving St Louis,' said Mike. 'We just love it there so much.'

Famous last words!

## Further confirmation

That was on the Tuesday. Then on the Wednesday the Lord spoke to Mike in a very unusual and dramatic way. He was told quite clearly that he was to move to Kansas City! In spite of such remarkable confirmation Mike really did not know how to proceed from there.

They returned to St Louis and for three months remained sitting quietly and simply waiting. At last in September Mike got round to sharing it with the elders. They were a little confused but they had all heard, or heard about, Agustine's prophecy and felt that with such clear confirmation it must indeed be God calling after all.

So very soon after, in obedience to this strange and strong call, Mike and Diane, their friend Bob Scott, and a few others, all sold up and went to plant a new church in Kansas City. In their prayers together they felt they should ask for a building in the south of Kansas City, one that would seat

700 people. Their search seemed frenzied and frustrating. They managed to look at twenty-eight places in four months but it appeared there were no such buildings available to them: nobody would believe they could raise the necessary rent. When it came to the interview with the agents the dialogue soon became all too familiar and the outcome almost predictable.

'How many church members do you have?' the agent would ask.

'Hm, well, we've got about eight people in total committed to this,' Mike would reply.

Roars of laughter all round followed as the agent closed his book, bringing another interview to its fruitless conclusion.

## A building at last

Then at last they found someone who owned a suitable building and was willing to trust them. Without further ado Mike signed the contract. He was told he would need to put down $21,000 by Wednesday.

'No problem,' Mike heard himself saying. 'We can get that all right.' He was thinking, 'I will have to get Bob Scott to sort that out – he's always so good at finances!'

He went off and found Bob Scott.

'We've got a place at last!' said Mike enthusiastically.

'Have you? How much?' was Bob's immediate reply.

'Bob – why all this concern about detail?'

'How much?' demanded Bob insistently.

'The rent is $8000 a month. But don't worry! I am sure we'll soon get that together somehow,' said Mike.

'Yeah!' said Bob, looking resigned.

'One other thing though, Bob! We need $21,000 advance payment by Wednesday!'

There were five days in which to find it.

## Now for the money

They had no idea where it could possibly come from. Only the Lord knew and the eight of them went to him once more in prayer. They had committed themselves not to tell a single soul of their financial needs. It was so vital to have the Lord's seal on this venture. They all felt that either the Lord was going to destroy this thing outright or he was going to make it come to pass by providing the money.

Amazingly two different people came to visit them, having heard they were wanting to rent premises to start a church in town. They said they wanted to help. Between them they gave $20,000. By then it was Tuesday afternoon.

That night Mike had to fulfil a long-standing engagement to speak at a meeting in St Louis. He flew there and gave the address. Afterwards the treasurer approached him, saying, 'We do not normally give our speakers anything except their expenses and a little extra. We do not know why but we have a strong impression that the Lord is telling us to give you a thousand dollars.' They had known nothing about the urgent need of exactly that sum. The Lord had marvellously provided. Mike was excited as he returned to Kansas City giving glory to God.

## Egyptian retreat

Soon after this Mike had to fulfil another long-standing commitment to join a team of eight North American pastors conducting teaching conferences across India. At the end of that time the other American pastors flew off East. Mike's own travels led him via Egypt where he had a visitation from the Spirit of the Lord while kneeling in prayer on the floor of his hotel bedroom in Cairo. God then spoke to him in an audible voice — it was so clear that he said he could even hear the intonations of it.

The Lord's word to Mike was: 'I am inviting you to raise up a work that will reach to the ends of the earth.' On hearing this a great fear fell upon Mike and he began to weep before the Lord and a spirit of groaning and travail welled up in him.

The voice continued: 'I have invited many people to do this thing and many have said "Yes" [Mike was sobbing: 'Yes, yes Lord!'] but very few have ever done my will.'

Mike was still responding: 'Yes, Lord, yes!'

Then he heard the Lord say: 'This is very serious,' and outline to him how the work was to be done.

'Firstly it will be built on night and day prayer.

'Secondly it will be built upon holiness of heart.

'Thirdly it will be built on unwavering faith.

'Finally it will be built upon extravagant giving to the poor. [There was a reference to Isa. 58 in this].

'Besides the Lord Jesus himself, these four principles will be the foundations of this work.'

Mike was still weeping and saying, 'O Lord – yes – yes!'

The Lord continued: 'Guard your heart for if you lose this vision it will be your brothers who have stolen it from you – it will not be the world that does that. It will be reasoning brothers who do not know my ways that will try to take this thing from your heart. Guard your heart lest your brothers steal this from you. If this standard is upheld, which I am inviting you and your people to follow, you will fulfil a purpose that will touch the ends of the earth.'

It was not just the fact of the visitation; it was the magnitude of the vision and the standards of it that left Mike astounded. He has shared how, many times since then, numbers of well-meaning brothers in Christ, who have professed to be trying to help in the work, have assaulted and resisted those standards. Many good people have come and wagged their fingers at Mike, saying 'You are off your head!' and have left the fellowship. Mike has learned to understand the hard way what the Lord meant when he said 'Guard your heart'.

The word from the Lord had been crystal clear. These

God-given principles have since become completely non-negotiable as far as Mike is concerned. He says he will not even discuss them after that solemn warning to guard his heart.

## Agustine again

It seemed that no sooner had Mike returned to Kansas City than Agustine was back in town. It was still September – 1982.

'Are you going to go ahead with planting this new church?' he asked Mike.

'Yeah,' said Mike with a nod of his head.

'Okay,' said Agustine. 'Then the Lord has told me four things you are to hide in your heart which will be very important for you. The first two are really glorious and the second two are terrible!

'1) Multitudes of young people – thousands will be rallied to you.'

Mike nodded, 'That sounds great! What's the second?'

'2) In the days to come there will be a full manifestation of the gifts of the Spirit but it will be for an appointed time.'

'That sounds great too! What's the third?'

Agustine continued: '3) There will be a false prophet in your midst from the very beginning. If you are patient and discern him you will save the church great heartache. If you do not you will suffer many, many problems.

'4) Finally there will be resistance and misunderstanding. Do not lose heart.'

## Starting with prayer

Mike had started the new fellowship by summoning the little group together for regular prayer. They prayed every night for three hours from 7 to 10 p.m.; and they continued like that for eighteen months. After Sunday worship for the public had commenced they began meeting for prayer three times a day. The little group (between ten and fifty – the

Lord had told them not to number the people) was excited
and full of faith.

In January 1983 an excited Christian brother bounced up
to Mike, saying, 'Hey! There's a prophet by the name of
Bob Jones in Kansas City and he's been talking for ten years
about a group of people the Lord had told him were coming
to the south of Kansas City who would be led by a twenty-
seven-year-old man. [That was Mike's age at the time.] The
group would speak about intercession and revival. [That was
exactly what Mike was teaching on.] Your group is the group
God has told him about and he wants to come and see you.'

Immediately all the warning bells about the false prophets
began to ring and Mike responded: 'No! I'm not interested
in meeting him. Maybe some other time.'

A month or two later up came another brother well-
known to Mike Bickle and said, 'Hey! You must meet this
guy Bob Jones. I've been hearing about him for years. He
said that our group is the one the Lord has told him about
and he very much wants to meet with you for just a short
time.'

Mike felt that the sooner he could sort this 'false prophet'
business out the better and this time reluctantly agreed to
see him.

## Enter Bob Jones

It was 7 March 1983 when Bob Jones eventually got his foot
through the door of Mike's office. Bob was an older man
— between fifty-five and sixty — and as he entered he was
obviously sensing some kind of anointing from God in his
hands.

'Uhuh! Uhuh!' he muttered to himself and then looked
up, 'Yeah! This is the group. I've seen you!'

Not properly understanding what Bob was saying and not
wanting any 'false prophet' to get one up on him, Mike
replied quickly, 'Yeah! I've seen you too,' thinking of
Agustine's serious warning.

'I thought you probably had,' murmured Bob with disarming pleasantness. But he obviously had not understood what Mike was meaning either, in his excitement to meet the young man at last.

And Mike was soon finding it hard to understand what Bob was meaning too.

'I have come to get involved with a movement,' he said, 'which is going to become worldwide; which is going to touch the nations of the earth with such power and glory that it will go far beyond the book of Acts!'

Mike was startled. 'A movement?' he stammered quietly, quickly running through all the implications of this in his mind.

'Yeah! The Lord told me that you would not know anything about that yet. My first task is to get you to believe it because the sooner you do the more difficulties you will avoid.'

## The strange white horse

Like the ancient mariner in the famous poem, Bob then spent the next two hours with his eye fixed on Mike telling him of some of the visions he believed he had received from the Lord. Central to them, it seemed, was a strange white horse with a board on its back bearing a young man. The horse was plodding along the mountainside in a stream of fresh water about four inches deep. Bob Jones was behind it holding long reins, not so much guiding the horse but steering it back into midstream, to protect it from mad rabid dogs; these apparently were sincere men with false doctrine but being rabid they had a phobia of water and dared not get into it.

Bob Jones said he imagined the man on the back of the horse must be Mike himself. The Lord had told him he was going to deliver that young man! Bob understood that his role was to help preserve Mike from those mad dogs. He would be able to reveal them to him one by one.

How sad, thought Mike, that this man was a false prophet, because he liked him, but he knew he really had to be so careful as a new church leader in Kansas City – especially since he had been so clearly warned.

## Foretelling his own acceptance

Finally Bob Jones concluded: 'The Lord tells me that on the first day of spring when the snows melt we will sit around the table – and the Lord gave me the words "agape" and "koinonia" – and we will sit around the table and they will accept me!'

'Whatever is this man talking about?' Mike thought, and then aloud he asked, 'Who will accept you?'

'They will,' replied Bob.

'And who are "they"?' Mike questioned.

'Well, you guys will!' said Bob.

Mike was now sure that this must be the false prophet. It was all so clear, he thought. But Bob was still rambling on.

He said, 'Let me tell you again. Last September, 1982 – six months ago – the Lord told me that on the first day of spring when the snows begin to melt the group will finally receive me.' He was obviously very earnest about being accepted.

Mike was thinking fast. The winter was already over. They were into sweltering heat and everyone was saying that spring had come early. Whatever was he on about? Anyone who prophesied his own acceptance had got to be a false prophet! Mike was certain.

As Bob was leaving he turned at the door with a throwaway postscript, 'Oh, by the way, the Lord has told me to tell you these four things but he said that you would already know them:

'1) Thousands of young people will be rallied to you.

'2) You will see a full manifestation of the gifts of the Spirit among you.

'3) There will be a false prophet in your midst from the beginning.

'4) There will be major resistance to you and misunderstanding but you are not to lose heart.'

'Hay-yay-yay!' gasped Mike, flinching on the horns of this fresh dilemma. 'However could a false prophet tell me that?' It was exactly what the Lord had already told him through Agustine!

# 6

# Beware the False Prophet!

The first time Bob Jones came to the Kansas City Fellowship church after that strange meeting a woman in the congregation breezed up to Mike saying, 'See that guy,' pointing to Bob Jones, 'he's a false prophet.'

'Yeah! I know,' said Mike, 'I'm watching him carefully.'

Later another person came up and singled out Bob.

'See that man over there? He's a false prophet.'

'Yeah! Thanks!' said Mike, 'I've got my tabs on that guy – don't worry!'

Without giving further details Mike said later that, unwittingly, he was in fact meeting regularly with a false prophet (he has never revealed publicly who this was) and there he was watching for an excuse to throw out a genuine one – for that is what Bob Jones turned out to be.

## The poor farmer's son

Bob Jones was born of humble parentage, the son of an illiterate 'cotton cuttin'' sharecropper, and raised in the 1930s among the cotton fields of Gravely, Arkansas. His spiritual nurture had been in the Baptist church there but he had had no real spiritual experience. He was experienced in other ways and had become quite a talented thief early in life.

At about the age of nine he experienced his first supernatural visitation. Ambling along a dusty track one day he suddenly saw an angel on a white charger coming towards him. He says it was Gabriel. The angel stopped right before him in the middle of the track and taking out a large silver trumpet he put it to his lips and blew. The angel then turned, looked straight at Bob and disappeared.

Paralysed with fear, Bob stood transfixed where he was for quite a while before turning tail and running for home. 'I thought he was calling me to die and to give up sin and I didn't want to do either,' said Bob. There was no one he felt he could talk to about that experience. He never mentioned anything about it to anyone until after his conversion to Christ years later.

When he was thirteen he had a second visitation; this time in a cotton field at the time of cotton picking. He was walking along the track when he heard his name called. He did not know how he knew but he knew it was the Lord calling him. Again he related the visitation to death, which he now realises it was − though not quite as he imagined: rather a death to self and rising to Christ. Once more he was filled with terror and rushed for home. The call was still not welcome.

## Out of body experience

Two years later he had a further mystical experience of great significance. He was taken, it seemed, out of his body and brought before the throne of God. The glory, the piercing light that went right through him and showed up in detail everything that he saw there, so terrified him that it took him about three months to recover − he shook so much. He thought that to see what he had seen he should have died and only the presence of an angel standing in front of him protecting his eyes enabled him to survive. When he came back into his body he was still hurting from a burning feeling within his very bones; the fear of the Lord was so awesome to him that his main desire was to get as far away from it as he possibly could.

He knew that what he had seen was the real thing but he

still did not realise that it was God's call upon his life —
or rather he did not want to realise it. He struggled hard
to forget. Striving to find peace in sin he ran away from
God.

## Running away from God

When the Korean War came Bob Jones joined the US
Marine Corps, where he soon became involved in drunken
brawls, fist-fights and gambling. 'I had no trouble at all
making grades' (getting promotion), said Bob. 'They sort
of approved of what I did.' Once a man fired at him at point-
blank range but the revolver failed to go off. A fist-fight
ensued and he beat up his opponent. Afterwards a friend
picked up the gun and fired it at the ceiling to see what was
wrong with it. It went off! Bob realised that his life had been
spared. In another brawl at Santa Monica every marine got
hurt except Bob. He knew then that there must be Someone
protecting him and he was still running away from him.

All this time Bob was leading his marine companions into
sin and himself into ever-deepening misery till eventually he
left the Corps. He and his wife Viola started to run an illegal
liquor store in the 'dry' State of Oklahoma where they made
a lot of money. His dream was to buy himself a big bar in
the middle of town and retire. But it all came to nothing.
At thirty-nine he was worn out. Sleepless nights and a
godless life had left him exhausted. His own comment in
retrospect, 'The damned can't rest', summed up those
wearisome days.

## Veterans' Hospital

Finally he went to a doctor who put him on drugs but could
not cure him. He was facing a complete breakdown. His
family had moved to Kansas City when he was still in his
teens. Now he was sent to the Veterans' Hospital in Topeka
nearby, where he was treated by a Christian doctor.

'I am taking you off dope,' he said.

'But doctor,' pleaded Bob, 'I can't live without it.'

'Oh yes you can, if you are going to live at all!' he insisted.

It seemed like hell to come off those drugs. All Bob could do was to pace the corridors of the hospital throughout the long nights. His hands were shaking continuously and involuntarily. One night his doctor saw what was happening and said: 'If I tell you to do something that will stop that shaking will you do it without question?'

'Yes-sir!' said Bob eagerly.

'Come with me,' he said and led Bob trembling along the corridor to the cleaning cupboard where he took out a mop. 'Now,' he said, 'every time you shake I want you to mop the floor.'

Bob began to protest, 'Me mop the floor?'

'Yes,' he said, 'mop the floor!'

Bob relates the story himself. 'I had never done anything like that before in my life but I found that when I began to mop the floors the shaking began to subside. I did it for days from about midnight to six o'clock in the morning.'

Then a friend sent him a book on Psalm 23 and as Bob read it he realised that he was terrified of hell. He began to cry out to the Lord for help. At about three o'clock one morning he knelt beside his hospital bed and repeated the psalm. As he did so he sensed a demon at his bedside speaking to him: 'Everyone has mistreated you in your life. No wonder you are like you are. You deserve to get even with them. Here is a list of twelve people that are responsible for your being here. Why don't you run away tonight and kill them and then come back? You are in the crazy ward anyway and you're going to be here for the rest of your life. They won't do anything to you.'

## Discharged at last

Immediately Bob cried out, 'Help me, Lord Jesus! Help me!'

Then the Lord came to Bob and said to him, 'I can't help

you Bob, until you forgive those people who have hurt you.'

So Bob proceeded to forgive them one by one and then he passed on to others the Lord was bringing to mind. He went back into the past as far as he could remember.

Then the Lord said to him, 'One of your greatest sins is self-pity. You blame everyone else for your problems.'

He felt something strange beginning to happen to him. The next day he was singing and whistling! His doctor stopped him in the corridor and said, 'What's happened to you? Come and see me in my office.'

When he had heard Bob's latest news he said, 'I've just got one more little job for you. Tonight I want you to take charge of the padded cells!'

Bob said he was both surprised and disappointed as he was so looking forward to what he believed would be his first good night's sleep. But he did what the doctor told him to do. Next day he saw the doctor again, who said (to quote Bob reporting him), 'You handled that pretty well! Now get out of this place.'

### Back to church

As the doctor discharged him he told him how he and the church he attended had been praying for him. So Bob decided to go to his doctor's church and see what it was like. He found it was a Baptist church like the one he had gone to in his early childhood and he soon felt at home there. He began to read the Bible whenever he could. He wanted to co-operate with the Lord in every way possible but he still had no assurance that his sins were forgiven. 'Getting to that place where I knew I was saved was the hardest thing for me,' said Bob. Every time there was a gospel call in church Bob was on his way up to the front again to get saved. He was still reading his Bible fervently, day in and day out, and finally he found peace with God.

Bob was discovering a strange thing happening to him. Whenever people were praising God in church he would find himself knowing things which he could not naturally know – not just about people and things going on in church. Once he found himself 'knowing' that Patty Hearst, the famous newspaper publisher's daughter, who had been abducted by a weird political group, was going to be rescued within thirty days. He shared this with the church publicly. Within thirty days Patty Hearst was in fact rescued just as he had predicted.

## Disturbed by visions

The church accepted that this was a gift which he had and was not at first at all disturbed by it, though Bob admits he was rather frightened himself. He just kept praying for protection through the blood of Jesus as he had been taught to do in the Baptist church. Visions continued to be triggered off whenever the people raised their hands in worship, spoke in tongues or simply praised the Lord!

After Bob's 'final conversion' he was baptised in a lake on 6 August 1975. Some friends then came and told him they should now lay hands on him and pray that he might be filled with the Holy Spirit. Bob was none too enthusiastic and did not really see the point. But these were good friends of his and they had arranged to take him out for a meal afterwards so he submitted to their request, as he says, 'simply to pacify them'.

As they laid hands on him and prayed for him something warm suddenly started running down his head and his back and then his mind began filling up with a Technicolor vision and he was speaking in tongues. He saw a landscape with the sun setting over it like the last hour of the day and it was impressed upon him that soon it would be too late for any man to labour in the harvest fields. He sensed the Lord telling him to pray that he would send out labourers to work in his harvest field.

## Learning to prophesy

After that baptism and the laying-on of hands Bob was returning home in his truck when he felt the Lord telling him to prophesy against abortion.

'How do I do that Lord?' asked Bob.

'Just raise your voice and speak it out,' the Lord told him quite simply.

So he did just that and as he began to prophesy against abortion he could suddenly see it all happening and hear the mothers and babies screaming. Sickened by the awful horror of it Bob finished his prophecy with the words: 'As you destroy the firstborn and the fruit of the womb so you will be destroyed.'

Not surprisingly as he shared this with the churches he began to find himself becoming unpopular: 'Don't bring these awful prophecies here,' they said.

Bob was then given another prophecy – this time against homosexuality. He began calling up church leaders on the phone and telling them. As he persisted a demon appeared, speaking to him face to face. The demon told him that if he kept on prophesying against abortion and homosexuality he would kill him!

'But I told the demon to get lost – I'm doing the Lord's work,' said Bob.

The demon did not leave but changed tack with some subtle temptations until Bob picked up the phone and 'reported' the demon to a praying friend telling him just what the demon was saying to him. At this the demon disappeared.

## Enemy counter-attack

Shortly after this Bob and his son Robert were out spraying fruit trees – that was how Bob earned his bread and butter. On later reflection, Bob said, recounting the experience, he should have taken the devil's threat much more seriously. Five minutes after starting work he began to feel great pain from the waist down. Every muscle ached and he was gripped by violent cramp.

It was so bad he had to go home. When things got worse the doctor wanted to get him to hospital but Bob protested: 'No! I know what's wrong. If I am going to die I'm going to die! And if that's the case then I want to die at home!'

The doctor gave him some pain-killers. Bob took two but the pain intensified. Then he started to haemorrhage from the nose and mouth. Bob wrapped a towel round his head and fell back on to his bed. Then the pain was gone. 'Suddenly I was in a dark place — a cave,' said Bob. 'There was a crystal light at the end and I knew that it was the Lord!'

Bob thought: 'So the devil did kill me after all! How could he do that?' As he started walking towards the Lord another thought began to press upon Bob: 'Did I get my robe clean?' He looked to see and the robe was like crystal light. There were no spots or darkness in it. He began to cry, 'I'm coming home clean after all I've been up to in my past. Oh! Thank you, Lord!'

## How could the devil do this to me?

Then I asked the Lord, 'How could the devil do this to me when I was busy doing your work?'

And the Lord put his hand up and said, 'You go back and teach the leaders of the latter-day church the old leadership is coming to an end. A new leadership with a burden for holiness is coming into being to bring forth the Bride of Christ.'

'But Lord,' persisted Bob, 'how did the devil get me?'

By way of an answer several possible reasons came to mind. In the first place, he did not have the protection from others interceding on his behalf. Secondly, he did not have the covering of a local church leader. Finally, he was immature and had been rebuking the devil out of his own faith. Next thing he heard was the Lord telling him that he was sending him back!

## Back into his own body

Bob described how he returned to the room. His body was still there wrapped in the towel. He remembered thinking to himself, 'I don't want to go back into that body where I had so much pain.' Then he saw two large angels that were praying for him. And there was a dark angel behind them but they would not let it touch Bob so it left. The two angels were talking about a group of young people who would be setting up in Kansas City.

'When I returned to that body I thought that I would be healed,' said Bob, 'but I wasn't. The pain was as bad as when I left the body.'

The only relief that subsequently came was through other people's prayers. The more the saints prayed the better he felt. When prayer stopped the pain increased. He could 'recognise' people he knew in his visions who were praying for him. The pain seemed to intensify during the Saturday afternoon baseball match − very few people's minds seemed to be concentrated on prayer for Bob just then!

On the Sunday morning Bob was suffering acutely with his pains. Everything from his waist down had stopped working. It was still hell for him at 10.04 a.m. when all his friends were gathered in church. At 10.05 Bob suddenly felt normal. It just seemed as though he had never been ill! He got up immediately and went round to the Baptist church, to testify to their answered prayer and the healing power of God.

## Sin in the church

Bob began getting prophecies for his local church. There were some things even in Bob's home church which were very displeasing to the Lord. A number of the young people were falling into sin and Bob 'saw' through the spirit of prophecy that if they did not stop sinning some of them would die. He spoke to a number of individuals there by name.

'I'm warning you — a number of you will die if you do not repent. Satan wants to destroy you!' he told them repeatedly.

They took no notice. Within three months seven of the young people from that church were dead! This appeared to be the result of a variety of tragic, isolated accidents.

The church expressed great concern and called Bob to a leaders' meeting. Before they got round to telling him that they thought he had put a curse upon the younger people in the church, Bob was suddenly 'shown' a serious matter among the elders themselves.

'This elder,' he said, pointing to one of them, 'is committing adultery with that lady' (who was also present at the meeting). 'They will cause a lot of trouble here and divide this church and leave with some of the church's money!'

That was the last straw! The elders threw Bob Jones out. They would have done better to have listened to him. Within two months it all happened just as the Lord had revealed to Bob.

## New fellowship promised

Bob and his wife Viola now began to feel rejected. They had really loved that church. Many people there had been blessed through Bob's prophetic and healing ministry among them. Married women who had been unable to conceive until Bob had prayed over them had since had babies that Bob in a way regarded as his grandchildren. They meant so much to him. Some of his close relatives had become members of that church. He was soon desperate for some fellowship and was feeling very depressed. The word of the Lord came to him again: 'I am raising up a group of young people in the south of

Kansas City. They will not reject you — nor will they turn away from me!'

This left Bob searching the city and crying out to God, 'Will they ever come, Lord?'

And the Lord appeared to him again. 'They will be there by the spring of 1983 and these will be the signs. Before the snows are melted on the first day of spring they will accept you. They will be in the south of the city. They will speak about intercession and revival and they will be led by a twenty-seven-year-old man.'

Since Bob and Viola needed Christian fellowship they had to join another church meanwhile. Bob explained to the minister from the beginning that they were only there temporarily and told him about the prophecy and that they would be leaving in the spring of 1983.

## Checking out Bob's story

All this was corroborated for Mike Bickle later. After he had known Bob a couple of weeks Mike felt he ought to go and seek the minister of that church to check out about the strange prophet.

'Do you know a brother called Bob Jones?' asked Mike.

'Of course,' replied the minister. 'He was a member of our church for three years.'

'Do you think he is a prophet?'

'Oh, yeah! He sure is. I've never known anything like his gift in my life.'

'What kind of a guy is he?'

'He's a tremendous friend of mine.'

'How do you feel about his leaving you?'

'Oh, I'm quite at peace about that because he told us openly from the beginning — when he first came to us three years ago — that as soon as "the young people" arrived he would have to go off and join them. I'm right behind him because I am sure he is doing the will of God.'

Mike Bickle was still ignorant of much of Bob Jones's

background and he had to admit that he felt very wary about it all. He would have been wary anyhow but he felt that since he had had a personal word of warning from the Lord about a false prophet he had to be extra careful.

Now that Bob and Viola were worshipping regularly and happily at Kansas City Fellowship it was understandable that Mike should continue to keep a rather watchful eye on Bob.

# 7

# Calling the City to Prayer and Fasting

It was March 1983. Art Katz was in town. Piloted by a
friend, he had flown into Kansas City in a private plane.
Art was the author of a best-selling book called *Ben Israel*
where he tells his own story of being a Jew in search of
meaning to life which he finds eventually through faith in
Jesus Christ. Art and Mike were old friends and they had
been catching up with each other's news on the Saturday.
Art intended flying out early on the Sunday. Sunday came
but the weather was unsuitable for flying.

Art planned to make the best of the unavoidable delay.
He would now be able to visit the Kansas City Fellowship,
which he was glad to do. It would be an opportunity to
worship with them and talk to some of the congregation.

## Prophet greets special visitor

It was after the morning worship when Mike was engaged
in praying for the sick that he just happened to glance
across the church. There, to his great consternation, he
saw Bob Jones ambling towards Art Katz, who was sitting
at the back. Mike gasped inwardly. He had not mentioned
anything about Bob Jones to his friend. And there was
no way to warn him now. Whatever would Art think about
the members of the new congregation he was meeting?
He clearly would not be leaving Kansas City with quite
the impressions that Mike would have liked him to have!
'There's nothing for it,' thought Mike, 'I'll just have to

trust the Lord to sort it all out.'

By then Bob was already talking earnestly to Art. 'He is probably used to handling nutters in any case!' thought Mike. 'He will soon nail Bob as a false prophet. In fact this could all turn out to be a real help — having Art's wisdom on the subject.' Mike calmed himself with such reasoning and returned to his praying. A little later he glanced up again only to see they were still talking together! 'Whatever is going on?' he wondered. When Bob had finished, Art came over to Mike looking disturbed and asked rather intently, 'Who was that guy?'

'I don't think I really know,' Mike replied. Adopting a role of ignorance and intentional nonchalance he was plainly dissociating himself from any responsibility for the embarrassing report he thought he was about to hear.

## The secrets of my life

'That man is a prophet of God!' said Katz. 'He told me secrets of my heart which no man could possibly know!'

Mike suppressed a cry as if in pain. He just could not allow himself to be taken for a ride by a false prophet — wherever and whoever he might be. It was a long day for Mike as he continued to thrash the problem of Bob Jones over and over in his mind.

That same evening Art approached Mike looking extremely distressed. 'Mike, I'm burning up! I feel I'm about to have a breakdown. I must see that old man once more. I have to talk to him. I know it's late [it was 9 p.m.] but is there any way I can see him again?'

'I'll call him up and see.' Mike dialled and waited till Bob picked up his receiver. 'Hi! This is Mike. Bob, you know that guy from the church you spoke to this morning . . .'

'Yeah! I know him,' said Bob, adding, 'I've been waiting for you to call me all day!'

Mike silently gulped but keeping his voice low-key, he said, 'Hey! How would you like to meet with us right now?'

'I'd love that,' said Bob.

'Right!' said Mike. 'We'll be over straight away. It'll be me, Diane, Art, his pilot, Bob Scott and a few others — six or seven!'

When they arrived they all sat around talking and Bob began to tell Art some more things about himself. Suddenly Art stood up and pronounced: 'I don't care what kind of reproach you may receive, Bob. I will stand up and bear your rejection with you because you are a prophet of God!'

## A private and personal sign

As Mike was telling this story to the church, he shared with them in an aside something he said he had never told anyone before.

'This is such a dynamic thing! This centres around Pat who broke his neck playing football in High School in 1973. Many of you probably read about that in the newspapers at the time. It was all over the front pages and on the radio. I was then studying at Washington University. I quit soon after because I wanted to be committed to the Christian ministry.

'My father came up to visit me at the university and we had a very serious talk. He said, "Mike, we are in a difficulty. I won't be around for ever and your five sisters can't take on Pat. I know you love the Lord. I want you to make a covenant with me for all the days of your life. Will you vow before the Lord that you will take the responsibility for looking after Pat?" '

Mike did not hesitate for a moment.

' "Dad, I promise I'll do that," I said, "it will be an easy thing," and as I said that a phrase from one of the latest "hit" songs flashed into my mind: "He's not heavy; he's my brother and I love him so much!" I took that as a very precious word from the Lord to me and I have often turned it back to him in my prayers for my brother! "Yes, Dad,

I promise I will do that!'' I reassured my father.

'I had never told anyone about that special prayer — not even my brother or my wife, it was just such a powerful, personal thing for me. Before we got married when I was courting Diane I explained to her simply about my commitment to Pat so she would know what she was taking on.'

He says he had never mentioned that special prayer to anyone because to someone else it could easily sound so stupid.

## Round about midnight

As they were still seated with Art Katz around Bob Jones's table that Sunday evening talking, praying and weeping before the Lord, midnight came.

Bob Jones spoke: 'By the way, an angel of the Lord visited me last night and told me I was mistaken! I asked him, ''What did I get wrong?'' The angel said: ''In that vision of the white horse in the stream that young man was not Mike but his brother Pat.''

'The other day Pat asked me if I had ever seen him before and I said ''No!'' Last night the angel re-ran that vision of the white horse which I have already told you about. I had always thought that the young man I saw carried on that board on the back of the white horse must be you, Mike! But when the angel spoke to me he showed me that actually it was Pat who was being borne on the white horse. So I had in fact seen Pat before but mistakenly I told him that I had not.

'Last night in that same vision I saw you, Mike, and I made a comment to you about the heavy responsibility you bore concerning Pat and you replied: ''He's not heavy; he's my brother and I love him so much.'' '

Mike was visibly startled at those words and began to sob. 'You can have no idea what you have just said to me! Those were the very words that I had used in my secret covenant with the Lord over my brother!' he sobbed. 'Not one single person ever knew that! You must, indeed, have been sent from God!'

Dazed, Mike was pondering to himself, 'However would this day have ended if Art Katz had left early this morning as he had planned. None of us would ever have been here. God has certainly ordained this!'

## What day is it today?
Then Bob Jones suddenly intruded into his holy reverie and asked him, 'What day is it today?' Though Mike was lost in his thoughts and did not catch the question addressed to him there was an answer.

'I don't know. It's Sunday!' someone murmured.

'Think! What day is it today?' Bob pressed the question with unusual insistence.

'It's 21 March,' said Mike, getting back on to Bob's wavelength at last.

'Yes, it's the first day of spring!' said Bob. 'Why didn't Art Katz leave today?' He was pressing again for an answer.

'It was because of the snow storm,' replied Mike.

'Look outside!' said Bob. 'What's happening?'

'The snows are melting!' they chorused.

'Thus saith the Lord!' said Bob who now and again would fall back on the odd phrase from his favourite King James Version of the Bible. 'On the first day of spring, before the snows melt, you will accept me around the table. This night has been ordained of the Lord. Truly you must hear the word that I bring to you, for God wants you to believe these things.' They were certainly all 'believers' now all right.

They went on through the night worshipping and weeping before the Lord.

Bob said: 'There's a sovereign movement of God being birthed which will reach to the ends of the earth and the Lord gave me that very secret between himself and Mike, which no man could have known, to verify his prophecy.'

Finally Mike rose from his seat at last and embraced Bob, saying, 'Truly you are a prophet of the Lord!'

That was 21 March 1983.

## Comet surprise for scientists predicted

Then Bob reminded Mike what he had already prophesied across the city — that there would be a comet whose coming was totally unpredicted by scientists. This would come as a sign of God from the heavens of his promised moving upon Kansas City. Mike was still amazed and wondered, 'Could God really be so interested in the people of Kansas City that he would promise them a visitation of his Spirit and would deign to give us such a sign — a comet — as confirmation of that?'

Not everyone in the Kansas City Fellowship was happy about Bob's sudden recognition as a prophet of the Lord nor the leadership's preoccupation with his strange prophecies. There was a tremendous amount of rejection.

But then they could hardly have appreciated the sovereign way that God had brought Bob Jones across Mike's path and how Mike had been finally convinced. And because of Mike's own uncertainties about Bob Jones's prophetic authenticity he had not known what exactly to share with the congregation and when to do this. Besides, Mike had yet to learn how to blend the ministry of a prophet with his own public ministry of preaching, teaching and leadership. Public church gatherings were not usually the best places for communicating this kind of prophecy — often given in enigmas and parables. Such revelations needed weighing sensitively, interpreting wisely and applying appropriately.

Mike was still learning and has had much to discover the hard way. This experience, combined with the wisdom he has gathered through the study of God's Word, makes what he has to teach on this subject today tremendously helpful. Some of his valuable insights will be elaborated upon in a later chapter (p. 116).

## Call the solemn assembly

Now it was April 1983. The fellowship had been meeting to pray every single night for five or six months. It was a Wednesday night – 13 April – when the Lord spoke again directly to Mike Bickle. Not audibly this time but 'internally'.

God said: 'Call the people together for a solemn assembly. Call the people together to fast and pray for twenty-one days! This people in the heart of the nation will be like Daniel who, when the children of Israel were in captivity in Babylon, went on a twenty-one-day fast' (Dan. 10:2–3).

Mike Bickle understood that this was the key to the release of the children of Israel.

The words continued: 'There will be 500 people in this city. They will stand before God as Daniel did because there are promises for this nation as there were for the children of Israel. This nation is in bondage just like the children of Israel. And God wants to free this nation just as he did the children of Israel.'

He said, 'I am going to raise up a Daniel from the heart of this nation as I did from the children of Israel. Read on from Daniel Chapter 9! Five hundred people will come together and they will fast for twenty-one days and they will seek my face and that will be the beginning of my purposes in a new dimension for this nation!'

Mike was trembling – scared to the bone! However could he get up and say that? He was only a very young and new minister in town. He could imagine the charges of presumptuousness which would be levelled against him if he ever dared to do such a thing through a city-wide summons.

He told his wife Diane and shared his fears with her. 'Darling,' he said, 'God has just told me through the Angel Gabriel to call a solemn assembly from this city to fast and pray.' The Kansas City Fellowship was having regular Sunday meetings for 300 to 400 people by then and God had said there would be 500 who would respond to this call.

Mike finished by repeating what God had told him: 'You lift up your voice and I will move the people! Do it because you have no choice. This is a command!'

Diane was dumbfounded. She found it hard to make any suggestions that would help him. 'All I know,' she said, by way of consolation, 'is that if things go wrong I'm sure we can go back to St Louis!'

Mike was surprised to sense in his spirit that he was becoming a little more resolved on the matter. 'I'm going to give it a shot,' he murmured, as if to test his own reaction. 'If we are done in this city we are done, but I know I've got to do it if this is really God. I'll call Bob Jones in the morning.'

It was 14 April. He called Bob. 'Bob, I have not known you for long but I know you are a prophet of the Lord. I have had a very scary word from the Lord that you don't know about.'

'Yeah, I already know about it!' came Bob's calm, drawling reply.

'Amazed' was hardly the word for it – this was all just too bizarre for words to Mike!

Bob said he had already 'seen' it and pressed Mike to go over right away.

Mike grabbed a couple of witnesses to take with him and they jumped into his car.

## An enigmatic dialogue

When they reached Bob's home he came out to greet them all and then sat them down as Mike launched into what was on his mind.

'Bob, I really need a word from the Lord right now!'

Bob replied, 'I have the word from the Lord already.'

'What do you have?' asked Mike.

'I saw him,' said Bob.

'Who did you see?'

He said, 'You know who I saw!'

Mike replied, 'Bob, I did not see anyone. That's not how God spoke to me! Who did you see?'

He was feeling a little peeved and impatient with this cat and mouse approach. Each of them believed he had had a revelation from God but was using the other's revelation to confirm his own. It seemed important for each not to give too much away while hoping that the other would corroborate it through the recounting of his own revelation. Hence this frustrating, enigmatic, step by step kind of dialogue.

Bob said, 'I saw the Angel Gabriel.'

'What did the Angel Gabriel say?'

'He said: "Give the young man Daniel, Chapter 9, and he will understand!" '

'That's incredible,' thought Mike to himself. 'We really have got to do this thing after all – we've really got to summon a twenty-one-day fast.'

Aloud he enquired, 'Will anyone respond to the call?'

And Bob replied, 'He said there would be 500 people!'

The same number exactly that the Lord had said to Mike – 500 – it was truly the word of the Lord!

So Mike made a city-wide call for a solemn fast to begin on 7 May. Just as he had feared there was opposition: the pastor of a leading church in town publicly condemned the unknown upstart for his audacity and called upon the Christian public to mark his words concerning that young Mike Bickle: 'Five years to the day that young man's name will be a vilification in the church,' he announced. Mike found that kind of attack particularly difficult. Criticism from the world was predictable. Condemnation from leading men of God was totally unexpected. A gentle tut-tut in private from an older, more experienced Christian, yes – maybe. But not a public curse from a leading churchman!

## Tense time in the Spirit

The next days were spent tensely waiting. Then the days of prayer and fasting began. The first night more than 700 crowded in to the church. They knew that, because the building seated 700 people and many were standing. They could hardly believe it! The next morning there was even more unbelievable news. Bob Jones brought the papers to Mike and pointed to the headlines. A comet unpredicted by scientists was coming across the nation! (See p. 85.)

Mike gasped, 'The Angel Gabriel and a comet! Incredible! I can't handle this, it's too much.'

I asked Mike for details of that fasting and prayer and he told me that they prayed through non-stop from 6 a.m. to 12 midnight. One person after another would simply come to the microphone and commence praying. They found themselves praying for many things over and over again.

Reporting later on those three weeks of fasting and prayer, when sometimes nearly 1000 people were present, Mike says: 'That was probably one of the most horrible times of my life to be honest. We felt so weak and barren.' But he realised that that was exactly what the Lord was trying to teach them. God had spoken to them from 1 Corinthians 15:42, 'The body that is sown is perishable, it is raised imperishable; it is sown in dishonour, it is raised in glory; it is sown in weakness, it is raised in power . . .'

## Three months of drought promised

On the last day of the fast Bob Jones got up and proclaimed a message to the city and the state.

'As the Ark of the Lord was hidden in Obed Edom's house for three months and as Moses was hidden for three months in the cradle so also there will be the total withholding of everything for three months, although God will allow a little bit of liberty.

'In this city everything will be withheld. For three months there will be a drought. That's the sign! God has spoken! The drought for three months is because the people have rejected the call to fast – they have mocked God. But for three months there will be no rain – not till 23 August.'

Bob had given a specific date for the end of a drought which he predicted was about to begin.

This level of prophecy could certainly be nervy! Mike found himself becoming an expert weather watcher. The weather, of course, was soon a matter of widespread public concern. To quote Mike:

'Kansas City was known as the bread-basket of the world; it was the centre of grain farming, fanning out to a radius of 500 miles.

'For the whole of June there was no rain! It was terrible!

'For the whole of July there was no rain! It was terrible!

'No rain still during the first week of August or the second or the third. It was terrible! Bob Jones said the Lord had told him it would come on 23 August. We had all been poised since early dawn that day but by 1 p.m. there was still no rain. By six o'clock we were just resigned to wait for another day when suddenly it began. And did it rain? It poured! No man could have manipulated that. It just had to be God!'

## Three more years of humiliation predicted

For three months God had humiliated the city because it had mocked and ridiculed. But now for three years, God told them through Bob Jones, he was going to humiliate the Kansas City Fellowship. God always resists the proud. He had to teach these people he was choosing to use that his strength could only be made perfect in their weakness.

# 8

## Promise of Revival

After the three weeks of fasting and prayer followed by the
three months of drought the church braced itself for the
three years' humiliation. God would reveal to them their
utter weakness before he began to release his blessing
through them according to his promises.

The incredible signs God had so sovereignly bestowed
upon the leadership would serve as a wonderful preparation
for any sacrifice which he might require from them. Now
they tried to settle down patiently, resolving not to waver.
Nevertheless they viewed the three long years ahead with
a sense of awe and of their total unworthiness.

While 23 August found them all giving glory to God for
the coming of the rain on the day Bob Jones had predicted,
the month ended with their having to assure each other that
what they had witnessed had all really happened. By mid-
September they were doubting that the experience was true!
October began with some of them asking, 'Who was Bob
Jones anyway?' By November Mike Bickle had a bad throat.
The church was getting difficult. People were grumbling.

### Yet one more sign

On 7 November Bob Jones appeared at the door of Mike's
office announcing that he had another 'word'!

'The Lord says that you are an unbelieving people.'

Mike, relating this later, said that he had thought of
himself up to that moment as a very believing person!

'He says that he will give you yet one more sign!'

Mike sat back with a smile.

'I love this. What is it?'

So Bob continued: 'The Lord says that on 15 November the word of the Lord will come to you in such a way that you will not waver in unbelief again. He says that he wants his people to believe so that his people are willing to make sacrifices for him.'

Mike: 'What's it going to be?'

Bob: 'It will be straight from heaven!'

Mike, somewhat cynically, 'That sounds exciting! I have not had too many of that kind of experience! It would seem that either I have to go up to heaven or someone has to come down if it's to be straight from heaven!'

Bob: 'Sounds something like that to me too, though you never know with these prophecies!'

## An appointment with God

November 15 arrived — the big day! Mike was sitting waiting, not really knowing how to approach such a prediction. Never before had he had to await a divine ministration of this kind. He tried praying, 'Here I am Lord,' and so on, though he felt the Lord would know that anyhow! He found it difficult to stay sitting for more than twenty minutes or so. He frequently got up to serve himself a Coke or something of the sort. He lasted out as long as he could and then gave up. It had not worked!

It was night time and he happened to spot a book by Howard Pittman, a Baptist preacher. Someone had sent it to him but he had never had time to read it. Pittman had been a policeman for thirty-five years and after retirement had opened an orphanage. In August 1979 he had had a death experience in the local hospital emergency ward which lasted from the Friday to the following Monday. During that time his spirit left his body and he found himself standing before the Lord. Pittman heard himself saying, 'Lord, I have been faithful to you all my days and I want my life back again. I have orphans in my care. I have faithfully preached the gospel. I regularly gave out tracts,' and he reminded the Lord also of many other good things he had done.

## Weekend in eternity

Howard Pittman stood before the Lord in his spirit for those four days, intermittently passing in and out of death in that emergency ward. Suddenly he heard the Lord addressing him: 'Your life is an abomination to my spirit!' In his mind Howard Pittman was saying, 'Lord, that can't be true,' and each time he protested the word of the Lord came thundering back to him with awesome wrath: 'Your life is an abomination.' Six times he heard the Lord repeating those terrible words until he finally knelt down before him and said, 'Holy Lord, forgive me. I've been a proud and arrogant man. I've done all these good works in my own name.' The Lord replied, 'That's true! I will forgive you and I love you very much. I ordain you, my son, to take a word to my people for these days.' He gave him a five-point message.

## The church that made God sick

Two of these points seemed especially relevant to Mike Bickle that night. One was that he was to tell the people that this was the Laodicean age and he would spit the Church out of his mouth because it was neither hot nor cold. He could find hardly a pure thing in the Church today – 99 per cent of the Church would have to change radically! The Lord explained to Howard that the reason he had wounded him was that his brothers would try to steal this message from his heart. 'You must know,' said the Lord, 'that it is I who am speaking to you and that is why I allowed you to experience my wrath.'

The other point was that Howard was commissioned to go and tell God's people that signs and wonders would begin occurring increasingly, and they would be greater than anything the early apostles ever witnessed. Howard had a strong theological objection to signs and wonders and protested. The Lord said: 'You are greatly mistaken for I will manifest my glory on the earth. Go down now for an appointed time and teach my people these things. Mark the date for on this day I am going to begin to enlist my soldiers for the Lord's army.' (This sounded very much like 'Joel's army' which Paul Cain had talked about.) 'I want you to mark the date,' he continued. 'On this very day I am going to begin the slow process of vomiting my Church from my mouth.'

The Lord said: 'Go and tell the brethren to be patient for though it will begin in my heart there will yet be a season of waiting and they must not grow weary, because it is I the Lord who am doing this.'

### That was it!

As Mike Bickle was reading, he thought, 'It all sounds just like us here.' He began checking the dates. Howard Pittman's death experience was in August 1979. The 'solemn assembly' for prayer and fasting in Kansas City began on 7 May 1983. The comet came on 7 May 1983. He double-checked the date the Lord had told Howard Pittman to mark – the day was 7 May 1983! Mike looked up. 'Oh, my God! – this is the revelation!' All the time he had been thinking that he must have missed it.

He looked up to heaven: 'Lord, how could this be? It's amazing! You sent Howard Pittman on ahead of time so that his testimony could be a confirmation of your other prophecies to me when I came to read his book on this day – 15 November!'

That was the sign from heaven which the Lord had told Bob Jones Mike would receive on 15 November so that he, the leader of the Kansas City Fellowship, might never again doubt God.

'My purposes are established,' the Lord declared plainly to Mike, whether in a vision or simply to his thoughts (he does not say), and went on, 'I am moving on the earth. This commenced on 7 May 1983. Tell the nations of the earth!'

Mike was shaking his head in awesome wonder. 'God! Why do you want these people so much to believe this?'

'So that they might be patient and understand the gravity of it,' came the solemn reply.

Those three years of waiting ended on 26 May 1986.

## Angels overheard

Way back in the mid-1970s Bob Jones had a vision, which has already been referred to, where he overheard a conversation between two angels.

One said, 'You know the Lord is going to move powerfully over this generation.'

The other replied, 'Oh! Is that so? When is the Lord going to move and where?'

He heard the first angel say: 'He's going to begin a mighty work in the midst of this city which will move to the ends of the earth. As this part of America is the bread-basket of the world in the natural so also it shall become the bread-basket of the world in the spiritual.'

The second angel asked, 'How do you know?'

And the first replied, 'There are a number of signs.'

(Bob felt these signs were in fact being given to him in this strange way. They are significant for the story now.)

'1) There would be 50,000 people gathered in the Lord's name as one sign.

'2) There would be a further gathering of 500,000 as another sign.

'3) Another sign would be the eruption of Mount St Helens on the north-west coast of the United States.

'4) Another sign would be worldwide famine.

'5) The Lord would raise up faithful and mature intercessors from Kansas City.

'6) Teams would go out from Kansas City to many places.'

(Mike Bickle is always careful to stress how the Lord has shown them that theirs is not by any means the only centre which God was committing himself to use in this way. And there was going to be a lot of cross-pollination between the centres. There could be no room for pride. One of the marks of the Lord's army would be that its soldiers were humble. There were many streams which flowed into the river, which made glad the city of God — and the KCF was just one of them!)

'7) A great explosion of light would go out from this city.' (Bob was shown a flash of brilliant white light exploding in the heart of Kansas City and out to the nation and it was impressed upon him that this would be the sign for the fulfilment of this prophecy.) 'The movement will have global significance like the flash of an atomic blast which occurs even though multitudes may not see it.'

## No one believed him

Bob Jones began to share these visions round about; and this was before the Kansas City Fellowship had arrived in town. No one could understand what he was talking about, and since he had not fully comprehended them himself this was not surprising. 'There will be 50,000 gathered in the Lord's name, then 500,000,' he boldly proclaimed. People thought he was mad. What Bob did not know was that there would be a time-lag before this happened as is so often the case with prophecy. In fact 50,000 did assemble at a large charismatic conference in the Arrowhead Stadium— Truman's Sports Complex — at Kansas City in 1977. Flowing out of that celebration 500,000 met in Washington three years later.

Most people had forgotten Bob's prophecy by then, but Bob himself was very excited when the 50,000 gathered in Kansas City, and most perplexed when the newspapers reported a crowd of only 350,000 at Washington!

He complained to the Lord about the lesser numbers, 'What went wrong, Lord? I missed it!'

But the Lord answered, 'Who do you believe, Bob, the newspapers or me?'

The other signs have been fulfilled – the eruption of Mount St Helens, the tragic famines and the raising up of intercessors in Kansas City.

## Noel is coming!
One Tuesday night in 1984 Bob Jones suddenly announced at the prayer meeting that Noel was coming! No one had any idea what it meant and the leadership pressed him for further details. But Bob said that that was all the Lord had told him to say. There were plenty of jokes going the rounds after that. Did it mean Christmas was coming? What else could it be?

On the following Friday Mike was at a pastors' fraternal, where he was surprised to meet a South African named Noel who turned out to be a pastor working on the other side of the city. The two had never met before. Noel had a tremendous burden for intercession and revival which matched Mike's exactly and so it was quite natural for them to want to meet again. They did so that night after the KCF time of intercession, which ended at 10 p.m.; Mike took along one or two other friends and they shared their common interest in prayer and revival, talking well into the night. Mike was so fascinated that he suggested, to Noel's surprise, that they meet yet again the next day and Noel agreed.

## Mississippi sign confirms promise of coming revival
As they were chatting together again the next morning Mike felt it appropriate to share the vision that God had given him through Bob. He explained about the white horse in the stream of water four inches deep. (The white horse

always appeared to symbolise the corporate work of God in Bob's vision.) Bob had seen this stream turn into a flood and the Lord had told him that once there were 500 committed Christians in the Kansas City Fellowship (by then meeting in their new Grandview Worship Centre) there would be an explosion of membership into 5000. They now had 1500 people regularly attending worship, but there were not yet 500 actually committed members.

The prediction was that once they had the 500 the flood would come instantly and in one hour they would be 5000. The prophet was shown that the majority of the added 4500 would be leaders and lapsed Christians who had fallen away over the past twenty years or so. They would be those who had had a clear call in the 1960s, 1970s and 1980s and had since lost it or fallen into sin and unbelief. God was going to show mercy on them. It was almost as if they had been prepared and were in waiting. The 4500 would quickly be mobilised into new wineskins that would be capable of containing the new wine: the new converts. So the first outpouring would not primarily be to bring in new believers but to restore old ones who would constitute the leadership for the new wineskins. Mike remembered that when Bob passed all this on to him, he had added matter-of-factly, 'The angel said: "That's the strategy! The sign will be 'Mississippi'!"'

In that vision the Lord had revealed that the numbers would increase from 500 to 5000 by multiplication; then 5000 to 10,000 by addition; then 10,000 to 15,000 by addition; 15,000 to 20,000 by addition; and 20,000 to 25,000 by addition. (A strange way of saying the numbers were going to increase. It would have seemed simpler to say from 500 to 25,000!) Mike and Bob were intrigued by the sign 'Mississippi'. They looked it up in every book they thought could give them a relevant clue. Mississippi, Mississippi! Whatever could it mean?

Then one day Bob Jones came into the prayer meeting

waving the latest edition of the *Kansas City Star*. There was the sign they had been waiting for. Headlines: FLOOD STRIKES JACKSON, MISSISSIPPI. 5000 PEOPLE SUDDENLY UPROOTED! The next day they read that the flood had affected 10,000 and then the next day 15,000. This indeed seemed to be the sign all right! The prophecy was beginning to make sense.

The leadership at Kansas City now felt sure God was preparing them for some very significant advance for the Kingdom of God. Mike was wondering if God might be calling Noel to join them in leadership for this but he needed to be especially cautious in view of the Lord's personal warning to him. There would have to be some very clear indications from the Lord. Was this the Noel of that enigmatic pronouncement earlier in the week when Bob had said, 'Noel is coming!'

## Major-General Alexander

Noel then shared with Mike a remarkable vision he had had from the Lord which was very precious to him and seemed to fit in with what Mike had been talking about. He was in Colorado. He felt the Lord calling him to spend time with him in prayer. It was way into the night. Then the Lord told him to stand up and look to the north. He asked Noel what he saw.

'I told him I saw a valley full of thousands and thousands of lilies.'

'He said, "They will be your inheritance. Those blooms represent the souls you will bring to me. Now look to the south! What do you see?" '

Noel looked at another valley stretching away in the distance and again it was just full of thousands and thousands of lilies.

'These are the souls you will also bring to me!'

When Noel heard that he just wept and wept.

As Mike was listening to this he marvelled and praised God. He said, 'I must take you to meet Bob Jones right now.

I'll call his number. I can almost guarantee that he already knows we are coming.'

He called Bob on the phone to check that he was in. 'Hello Bob! I have got a man here . . .'

'Yeah! I know. Bring him over.'

Mike was not even surprised any more. They were soon at Bob's house.

'Yeah! You're the one,' muttered Bob as they entered. 'What's your name?'

'Noel Alexander,' said the South African.

Bob was rummaging through his rather grubby pile of papers — a collection of some twenty-five of the thousands of visions he had had from the Lord that he had specially written down. These were the ones which were still puzzling him.

'Here we are!' he said. 'Vision of November 1976: when Major-General Alexander is released then it will be a new step in God's purpose for this move!'

Bob had kept the vision from 1976 to that date in 1984. He now addressed Noel: 'God wants me to put a mirror in front of you. When I tell you something you will see your life and when you see your life you will know that God wants you to understand something more that I will show you.

'The Lord showed you to me as a man who stood before a valley of many, many flowers — he showed you multitudes of flowers and he has told you that this represented your inheritance as part of his body.'

Though God had only told this to Noel recently, he had revealed to Bob, as far back as 1976, that 'Major-General' Alexander would be used to bring thousands and thousands into the Kingdom of God. Bob said he had never been able to figure out the 'Major-General' bit. He had a friend at the Pentagon whom he had asked to identify this Major-General Alexander for him but according to his friend there was no general in the US army of that name. Perplexed, Bob had stored the vision away for its proper time.

## Thirty-five apostles

Bob then proceeded to tell them about a vision concerning thirty-five apostles God was raising up from Kansas City. Four of these were carrying the Ark of God. Bob felt a great desire to share in the privilege of bearing the Ark like those apostles but the Lord said 'No!' He felt so emotional about not being permitted to 'bear the Glory', as he put it, that he almost missed the rest of the prophecy. The burden of it was that there would be thirty-five apostles released from Kansas City.

When Mike Bickle retold this story to the church he explained that there could be different levels of apostleship. Those Jesus appointed had to have seen him in the flesh and had to have done the signs and wonders of an apostle. Mike admitted to the possibility of a different level of apostleship without detracting from the uniqueness of those chosen by Jesus in the gospels.

## No careless choices

According to Bob, the Lord had told him in July 1984 that He would reveal something about leadership to Mike face to face. Mike found the prospect awesome – he had never been through something quite like that before and was not sure how he would handle it. A month went by. It was the middle of August. Out of the blue Mike received a long-distance telephone call from Agustine.

'The Lord said to tell you that tonight he has an appointment with you. He is going to take you to the Third Heaven to speak with you face to face. Were you expecting him?'

'Well, as a matter of fact I was kind of expecting something like that!'

'Well, it will happen tonight! Goodbye – and have a good night!'

Down went the receiver! Mike hung up, pensive and slightly trembling.

The prayer meeting had ended at 10 p.m. and Mike was already tired and went to bed. At 2.15 a.m. the Lord came and it seemed to Mike that he was being taken out of his body. He found himself lifted up into a court room where God solemnly warned him in a terrifying, thunderous tone: 'Young man! If you are impatient, particularly in the realm of endorsing the leadership of those who will want to be identified with this movement because they only want to get something out of it, you will cause great harm and turmoil to many people.'

Mike was then transported back into his body leaving him wondering whatever it could mean. He was thinking that the Lord must have detected a tendency in him to want to hurry things up. He felt awful. Then as he was lying on his bed he found himself suddenly being taken up again. This time the Lord showed him a number of apostles whom he could not easily count as he was viewing them sideways on (but Mike said they could have equated with the thirty-five Bob had mentioned concerning a previous vision.)

The Lord said: 'That is the number of apostles who will come forth from this city!'

## Pat's strange heavenly visitation

Later in August 1984 Bob Jones came up to Mike. 'Oh, by the way, I have a prediction for you. A young man is going to have a vision very soon. It will lift you high off the ground. You will hold on to him and not let go.'

What young man could be going to have a vision that could cause Mike to leap up like that, he wondered. He went home rejoicing. Once in the house the phone rang. It was Agustine. 'Mike! God is going to visit your brother Pat tonight! He will show him that he will heal him!'

The Lord did indeed visit Pat during the night. It was at 4.03 a.m. on the Friday. Pat was wide awake when in what seemed like a trance (cf. Acts 10:10) the Lord appeared and he was terrified. 'I have come. For eleven years I have not dealt with you,' said the Lord. It seemed slightly enigmatic. Pat came out of his trance and lay on his bed still in great fear. He had clearly not been healed. That morning he called Mike and asked him what it meant.

Whilst Pat was still on the line, Agustine (who only knew directly from the Lord what had happened to Pat that morning) called Mike on another line. Unable to reach him, Agustine left a message: 'Regarding Pat's visitation last night, look at Acts 3 where you will see that the key miracle that opened up the city of Jerusalem was the healing of a cripple, and then at Acts 14 where another cripple was healed and this second miracle opened the door for the gospel to enter at Lystra. The Lord has called Pat and told him that he is going to heal him and this will be the key for the gospel to the whole of Kansas City.'

Mike was thinking fast. God had made Pat to be a sign to this city. Most people would have forgotten the story of his accident and subsequent testimony by then, but it seemed they would soon have cause to remember it.

## Meeting with Paul Cain predicted

On one occasion after they had come to know each other well Bob came to Mike and asked him, 'Are you picking anything up from the Lord?'

'No,' said Mike, 'not that I am aware of.'

'Well,' replied Bob, 'am I in sin? Can you see anything about me? Am I quenching the Holy Spirit?'

'No! Really, Bob, I am not aware of anything. Why?'

''Cos the Lord has shut the whole thing down!'

'Whatever do you mean, Bob?'

'Well, I haven't seen a vision in two nights!'

Bob was used to seeing five or six visions on any average night.

Before the end of the year, however, Bob Jones was getting a number of particular revelations about another older prophet somewhere whom the Lord was going to bring across his path, and though Bob was not given his name the man became clearly identifiable as Paul Cain. They had never met. Mike was intrigued.

In September the same year Mike was giving a lift to Agustine, travelling from Arizona to a conference in California organised by the Vineyard Ministries International (where incidentally I later realised I had first met Mike myself). On the way Agustine mentioned that he knew of a prophet called Paul Cain who received very significant revelations from God. Of course Mike was fascinated to learn all he could about him in view of his beneficial experience of prophets by that time.

They happened to stop along the way at a McDonald's where Mike caught sight of a face he recognised.

'Hi,' said Mike, 'what are you doing these days?'

'Oh!' replied the man, Reid Grafke by name, 'I've just started working with Paul Cain in Dallas.'

Mike found the coincidence quite extraordinary and felt God alerting him that one day he was going to meet Paul face to face! He accepted, however, that God himself would arrange such a meeting his own way should that truly be his will. Mike was learning not to get ahead of God.

# 9

## Our Interview with the Prophets

Whatever were we visitors to make of all these visions and signs? Some had clearly been fulfilled in most remarkable ways and others predicting revival *en masse* still awaited fulfilment. It was fascinating, coming from our rather cynical culture, to meet so many people who seemed to accept so easily the whole dimension of revelation at this level. We could almost understand why they believed it, but for us outsiders, who had not been involved in the gradual, step-by-step process of a movement of God through revelation and the subsequent fulfilment of signs, the novelty was mind-boggling.

On the Sunday afternoon Mike Bickle had arranged for us to meet a number of the prophets in one of the church offices. I do not remember all those present, but besides Mike Bickle himself and Bob Jones I recall Jim Goll, John Paul Jackson, Mike Sullivant and David Parker. There were also others who were on the staff. We were grateful for this opportunity to meet in this relaxed way and the abiding impression of that meeting was the openness to God, the readiness to listen, the deference each gave to the others, and their submission to Mike's authority as leader.

We enquired how they had all come together. It was a matter of amazement to us that there could be so many prophets receiving such a high level of revelation from God who were all living in the same city and all committed to the Kansas City Fellowship. Most of them had found themselves rejected in their previous churches. Truly, as Jesus said of himself, a prophet has no honour in his own country (Matt. 13:57). It appeared that this coming together had been brought about through the Lord's direct overruling. Unbeknown to each other they had prayed and the Lord had told them Kansas City was to be a prophetic city and they had been drawn there by the Spirit of God like moths at night to a lighted candle. God had told them to get up and move to the land of the anointing and 'I will greatly bless you'.

None of them had been aware of the secular history of Kansas City, a book written about the year 1900 and handed down to David Parker through his family, whose subtitle 'Kansas – the prophetic city' had been given to it by the founding fathers. David had only recently noticed this and had communicated it to Mike and the rest of the KCF staff.

Humanly speaking, had it not been for the wise, gracious and thoroughly Bible-based leadership of Mike Bickle, they might well have had their prophetic gifting stifled to death. This, it now seems probable, is most commonly the case in the Christian Church.

There were several things, obviously, that we were wanting to ask these prophets, and perhaps the fact that there were four of us to put such questions and so many of them to answer meant that we did not find out all we wanted to know. Perhaps we never will!

## How are prophecies received?

Our first question was: How do prophets receive their revelations. Is it through the 'psyche' (soul) or the 'pneuma' (spirit)? This was important for us to clarify. For the average Christian the word 'psychic' is tainted by its association with the occult but in fact the Greek word 'psyche' is a wholesome New Testament word translated 'soul'. Such a good biblical word clearly needs redeeming today. The psychic centre in each of us seems to have a vital role to play in the area of revelation from God.

Then if occultists get limited communication from the powers of darkness on to the psyche, which some claim to be the case (though obviously such revelations, even when true, have an evil origin for evil objectives), then such a counterfeit must be matched by a genuine experience from God Almighty. Wherever there is the counterfeit there must be the genuine reality. No one would be deceived by a £13 note. It must clearly be false because there are no genuine £13 notes in circulation. But anyone might be deceived by a counterfeit £10 note.

The consensus of opinion among the prophets in answer to our question seemed to be that the psyche was involved in their visions. They were clearly neither embarrassed nor threatened in any way by our description of their gifts as psychic in the pure sense. Of course, this is an area where it is impossible to be anything but tentative because there has not yet been found any scientific way of distinguishing between soul and spirit. We cannot take a soul and preserve it in a test-tube, or a spirit and dissect it under a microscope. And who among those who might object to Christians using the term can prove in fact that occultists themselves really do operate through the psyche? Or who will argue that because spiritualists profess to operate through the spirit world we Christians must avoid the use of the word spirit in our religious experience or theology?

In so far as these prophets seemed to have had a large number of revelations which have proved in time to be true, have served the common good and been glorifying to God, their views were worth hearing. They seemed to have no problem in accepting the term psychic in this pure sense to describe one part of the process of divine revelation to human beings.

The human spirit is a channel which picks up spiritual transmissions from God or from the powers of darkness and these are reflected on to the screen of the psyche, the soul. The same TV channel can carry beastly cruelty, pornography or breathtaking beauty. The responsibility for the subject matter lies not in the channel itself but in the source of the transmission or the choice of the person tuning into the programme.

The antennae of the spirit appear to involve, among other things, possibly, the counterparts of the physical senses. The psalmist hinted at something of the kind when he said 'Taste and see that the Lord is good'. The transmissions are tasted, smelt, seen, heard and felt. For these prophets all the senses might be spiritually operative when they receive communication from God but probably most of them would major initially from one 'sense'. They stressed the need of training in this through constant use (Heb. 5:14). At the end of our session, when these brethren were about to prophesy over us, Bob Jones turned to John Paul Jackson and said: 'You had better start, brother — I can see the anointing on your eyes.' It was a strange expression to our ears, but even stranger, I had already seen the anointing on him with my own eyes.

To some God vouchsafed open visions where the picture or the word was very clear and at other times enigmatic speech, riddles and parables.

## How to be receptive channels

'Is there anything we need to avoid which might obstruct reception?' we asked. It was clear these men all had a supreme commitment to 'follow after holiness' and their comments would be most helpful.

John Paul shared how the Lord had dealt with him over a problem he had with false visions which came to him as flash-backs resulting from too much watching of TV. He said that for the prophetic ministry which God had given him the more television he watched the less true visions from God he could experience.

Bob Jones agreed that the Lord would not let him watch much TV either. 'I can't get into that fantasy realm — it cuts off my visions!'

They advised watching carefully against counterfeit visions of any kind. Someone mentioned alcohol as creating confusion, since when taken in excess people can begin to 'see' things: 'prophets . . . befuddled with wine; they reel from beer, they stagger when seeing visions, they stumble when rendering decisions' (Isa. 28:7). Great care was needful indeed about anything which distracted the heart and the mind from God.

Another problem they shared was the danger of confusion over revelations where the person receiving them had particularly strong opinions, prejudices or unresolved bitterness in certain areas. It was easy to distort such revelations and colour their own interpretations. Such revelations should be jettisoned.

Anyone professing to have a revelation from God needs to ensure that his/her relationship with God is good: 'I did not speak to them [says the Lord], yet they have prophesied. But if they had stood in my council, they would have proclaimed my words to my people' (Jer. 23:21−22).

## Do prophets ever get things wrong?

This led on naturally to our next question. We asked tactfully if any of them was ever wrong? I was thinking of the time when Bob had mistaken the identity of the person borne on the white horse — it had been Pat and not Mike as Bob had first thought. They all agreed that they had often been proved wrong. Sometimes their revelation was right but their interpretation or application was wrong. According to Mike Bickle, who confirmed that they certainly could be wrong, the problem seemed to be that they were right too often to be ignored.

In the Old Testament they would have been put to death for giving false prophecy (Deut. 18:20); but Mike pointed to the grace of God who had instructed simply, through New Testament revelation, that their visions and prophecies should be weighed by others (1 Cor. 14:29).

No one should act on one prophecy alone. If it came independently as a confirmation of something that God had already been speaking about in other ways it certainly would be an encouragement to proceed in that direction. There was always the further check that if it were right there would be peace of heart about it (Col. 3:15). But if the revelation is something completely new and out of the blue it is important to wait, watch and pray for further confirmation.

We asked them how they felt about getting things wrong. They all agreed that it could be humiliating. Nowadays they have learnt to offer their visions with some clear disclaimers to any idea of infallibility just in case anyone should want to assume a prophet could never err. But they still felt confused and sometimes rejected if they got it wrong. Sometimes, too, they thought they must be wrong and felt just as confused and rejected when they found out later that they had been right after all.

Bob Jones told of an occasion when he was at a meeting in his home church where there was a wonderful time of worship and praise, and the word of the Lord came to him: 'Macaroni cheese'!

He naturally hesitated about speaking out such a word as that; it was just too stupid! But the word kept pressing on him and eventually he summoned the courage to speak it out. When he actually did call it out the congregation laughed so much he was really embarrassed. To make matters worse the pastor, who was obviously embarrassed as well, made light of it by suggesting that Bob must be hungry! At this point a whole family got up and walked out, which only intensified Bob's discomfort. He went home to his favourite place with God, his woodshed in the garden, and repented.

It was several months before he heard the other side of

the story. An old saint of God, a widow who lived way out in the countryside, had a family of eleven. The eldest ten were all serving the Lord but she was very concerned about the youngest — still apparently a godless truck driver. She told the Lord in her prayers that she was getting old and she wanted some assurance from the Lord about this wayward son before she died.

She had heard of Bob Jones and decided to visit the church where he normally worshipped. She asked the Lord to give her a sign which only she would understand. When she got there that crazy word from Bob Jones was just the assurance from God she needed. She was quite appalled when everyone laughed as she felt this was a sign of disrespect for God's prophet and left with her family, both distressed and delighted. Distressed for the church. Delighted for herself. Her son's truck-driving was taken up with a regular delivery service for macaroni cheese! She could not have had a better coded word of encouragement from the Lord!

Failure was something which most of them had felt very acutely at first but were learning to cope with better. This was partly due to the warm and understanding fellowship of the other prophets, and partly to the very positive place being given to prophecy by the leadership. This meant that most of them now found they could cope much better with being shown to be wrong or even being misunderstood; but it was still painful.

## Are prophets born with the gift?

We wanted to know if they were all born with this gift. To our surprise we discovered that most of them now felt they had been called, like Jeremiah, from their mother's womb to their prophetic office. I have since talked to others with this gift only to find that often their offspring have had the gift also. (Such a discovery gives some insight into the comment of Amos who claimed he was neither a prophet

– not trained in any prophetic school; nor the son of a prophet – not born into a prophetic line (Amos 7:14). This could also explain why Paul seems to list prophecy as a natural talent in Romans (12:6–8) yet still refers to it as a spiritual gift in 1 Corinthians (12:10). This also helped us to see how those not born with the talent of prophecy could receive the gift of prophecy later in life.

David Parker seemed to be the only one among the prophets to whom the gift had come, or who discovered he had been given it, later in life. He had had an academic background and had at one time done some post-graduate studies at Regent's College in Vancouver. With faculty encouragement he had been tentatively feeling his way towards Cambridge to study for a Ph.D. when the Lord checked him.

He had told David that he was a good student but he was looking for good disciples. This had changed the direction of David's life. David, who was brought up in Kansas City, has since founded and leads the Northside Fellowship Centre (membership *c.* 250), which is one of the newer daughter churches of the KCF.

We then asked further how anyone who desired this gift might receive it. They said that such a person would need to make a commitment to getting it and really wanting it (1 Cor. 14:1); to pray for it and to work with others who had it. It was also possible for someone who had the gift to impart it (Rom. 1:11; 1 Tim. 4:14; 2 Tim. 1:6); but Paul's injunction to 'lay hands suddenly on no one' would also apply here. Where the gift had been ignored or unused for some time (as was probably the case with Timothy), it needed to be 'stirred up' again.

It was a great help, they said, if one could get to be with others who already had such an anointing 'as it kind of rubbed off on you' – it was like the mantle of Elijah falling on Elisha. Mantle prophets call forth other mantle prophets.

Finally, in using the gift some have just had to start 'in

proportion to faith' with an impression (Rom. 12:6). No wonder Wimber spells faith R−I−S−K! The only real way to learn is through the experience of stepping out − like Peter who actually got out of the boat and walked a few paces on the water. When the Lord told Bob Jones to prophesy against abortion Bob asked the Lord how he was going to do that and the Lord told him to start doing it right there, where he was, in his truck. This proved to be a vital step in the development of his prophetic ministry.

David Parker shared how he had longed to find an experienced teacher to help him become a prophet. As he was praying for this he had a vision of being in an old study with a teacher who went to his cobwebbed bookshelf to find something suitable. At last he took down a musty old tome entitled *The Ways of the Spirit*, which he handed to David. But it was not really a book at all − it was a scrap book − and inside were things like a piece of bandage, a snotty old handkerchief, a tear-stained letter and so on. He realised that the Lord was telling him that one could learn only by experience.

Prophecy, it seems, may be a natural talent for those who have been born with it (Rom. 12:6−8), but always to be exercised properly in God's service it must be 'in proportion to faith'. It is also seen in Scripture as a spiritual gift (1 Cor. 12:10), conveyed through the anointing of the Holy Spirit, and to be used for the common good. Finally, it seems that prophecy may also be imparted by another person who also has the same anointing (Rom. 1:11).

## Are prophecies always fulfilled?

'Do all the prophecies come to pass?' we asked.

'No,' they said, 'not all of them are meant to.'

Usually negative prophecies pointing to death and destruction are given to indicate what the enemy is specifically intending to do, and these are to alert the saints to prayer. Jesus saw that Satan desired to sift Peter as wheat, which looked like being a terribly painful ordeal for him, but Jesus prayed for Peter to protect him.

But sometimes there can be no doubt that it is God's clear intention to bring immediate judgment upon a nation or to terminate the life of an individual. The Lord made this clear through Jeremiah when he said:

> If at any time I announce that a nation or kingdom is to be uprooted, torn down and destroyed, and if that nation I warned repents of its evil, then I will relent and not inflict on it the disaster I had planned. And if at another time I announce that a nation or kingdom is to be built up and planted, and if it does evil in my sight and does not obey me, then I will reconsider the good I had intended to do for it. (Jer. 18:7–10)

The city of Nineveh was a case in point. The people repented and God withheld the promised judgment. That made Jonah angry. He felt that God's mercy on the Ninevites, once they repented, had undermined his own prophetic credibility. The Lord showed Amos that he was about to send a plague of locusts and a judgment of fire upon Israel. In each case Amos prayed the Lord not to let it happen and each time the Lord relented (Amos 7:3,6).

King Hezekiah was an example of God reconsidering a case in changed circumstances. God had warned Hezekiah through Isaiah (38:1) that he was to prepare to die but when Hezekiah prayed for a longer life, God gave him another fifteen years.

It is clear that the fulfilment of prophecy is not inevitable; usually it is conditional. Positive promises are often made clearly dependent upon one remaining faithful to God (Jer. 18:9–10), believing the promises and getting prepared for their fulfilment. Negative prophesying should be countered by repentance and prayer.

## Is prophecy linked with personal holiness?

Is there a link between the prophet's character and this ability to prophesy? Was there a need to attain a certain level of holiness before one could be anointed with this gift? There are instances in the Bible where men had prophesied who were either corrupt like Balaam (Num. 24:17; Rev. 2:14); childish and angry like Jonah (Jonah 4:9); or hostile to Christ like Caiaphas (John 11:50; 18:14). Our friends showed from the example of their own calls that God had anointed most of them in immaturity. The gift of prophecy was not contingent upon maturity or holiness but upon the sovereignty of God.

But they had no doubt that since major strands of their prophecy were concerned with justice and holiness – reflecting the character of God – he required a matching up with the prophets' own lives. As far as possible they should themselves be models of their prophecy and be seen to be worthy representatives of the author of the revelations. The fruit of their lips must equate with the fruit of their lives.

Had not Jesus said 'By their fruit you will recognise them. Do people pick grapes from thornbushes, or figs from thistles? Likewise every good tree bears good fruit, but a bad tree bears bad fruit. A good tree cannot bear bad fruit, and a bad tree cannot bear good fruit' (Matt. 7:16–18)?

# 10

# Leadership versus Prophecy

By this time I can imagine most church leaders beginning to wonder how they would ever cope with a prophet if one should show up in their congregation. It need not be difficult at all! Whenever I borrow someone else's car the first thing I want to know (assuming it is licensed, insured and roadworthy) is how to drive the vehicle: 'How do the gears operate and where are the brakes?' Once I know about these things, though I understand very little of the workings of the engine, I am ready to edge the vehicle out on to the road. My approach would be much the same about raising a prophetic ministry in the local church. Once a leader recognises the value of prophecy and understands how this ministry can be managed, even though he may understand very little of how it actually works, he is likely to be much more relaxed and to approach the subject more constructively.

## The dynamics involved

It is helpful to sketch out some of the basic problems so that the pastor, the people and the prophets can all understand the dynamics involved. It's probably a joke, because I never saw one on sale, but Mike says his tape called 'Insecure Pastors and Rejected Prophets' was a best-seller! The title neatly says it all. There is the potential in any emerging prophetic ministry for major tensions. The person sharing a prophecy is naturally concerned about being received and obviously feels in need of positive encouragement when he is risking his own reputation.

The pastor knows that he has to carry the can for any disorder and senses the need of the flock to be protected from ravening wolves or naïve ego-trippers. The average congregation has a great accumulation of wisdom and is both concerned about being taken for a ride and offended that anyone should imagine they are going to allow themselves to be duped. They are also worried that their minister is unaware of how things could go wrong.

Further, especially if the person prophesying is a good person with the best of intentions, the question of authority is posed. If the prophecy comes directly from God, should the prophet take over the church? Does the one who speaks *ex dono* have a higher authority than the one who speaks *ex officio*? Does the eye no longer need the hand? That was the kind of confusing misunderstanding that brought about Edward Irving's downfall in his famous London Presbyterian church in the early 1830s. Out of his deep humility he mistakenly assumed that those with gifts of the Spirit must in some way be superior to those with responsibility for government in the church.

## Governmental authority

But the duly appointed minister can never surrender the solemn responsibilities of his office otherwise there will be spiritual anarchy. There was an occasion when the apostle Paul said, 'I magnify mine office' (Rom. 11:13 KJV). There may be occasions when a church pastor has to do the same.

No prophet has been given that kind of authority over the church; he does not have governmental authority. He may have authority – God's anointing – to prophesy but if it is in the church then it must be under the authority of the leadership appointed by the church. The leadership may require him to desist from prophesying there at any moment and even forbid his prophesying altogether. Of course, the leader is accountable to God at all times for whatever course of action he may think it is right to take.

Not many prophets want to take over the leadership, but if they had real potential for church leadership they would not attempt to get it in that way. However, some leaders are prophets. We remember Moses who was both a prophet and one of, if not *the*, greatest human leader in history. Ezekiel was a priest besides being a prophet. And, of course, Jesus was a prophet too – *the* prophet (Deut. 18:18 and John 4:14).

Some embryonic prophets unwittingly crave public visibility and have endeavoured to get this from within a congregation for which they do not have responsibility and for whose upbuilding they have apparently done very little previously.

But should a leader ever feel a little insecure in the exercise of his office when confronted by a prophet who claims to have a message from the Lord (and there are often situations where a leader might easily feel threatened – especially where the situation is new and he has no precedent for dealing with it), he should always remember that he has the proper authority to lead the church and the prophet does not; indeed his conduct in a leadership role would probably prove very inadequate since that is not his particular gifting.

Too often the fact is that the pastor, initially unused to anything of the kind, perceives the prophet as a threat to his leadership and, as such, one to be snuffed out speedily in the name of decency and order. In which case, should he wield the sword of authority too heavily, he may cut out the prophet's tongue completely and annihilate the possibility of a prophetic ministry altogether.

Jesus said that he who receives a prophet in the name of a prophet receives a prophet's reward (Matt. 10:41). Many church leaders have no idea how to receive a prophet and would be totally ignorant of both the role and function of prophecy in the Church and the world today. They would

not want their ignorance to be exposed either. But where
can leaders possibly get positive help and enlightenment?
How can such a ministry be fostered? How can nascent
prophets be nurtured? They have no good models in their
particular ecclesiastical tradition to help them to foster
prophecy in the Church so one of God's gifts for the Church
is stifled and dies. The Church is much the poorer for it.
And as someone has wittily put it: 'If you don't have
prophets you suffer losses!'

## Limiting prophecy

It is probably best at first to limit prophecy in church to
the simple inspirational kind that we read about in
1 Corinthians 14:3 which is for edification, encouragement
and consolation. Other prophecy such as the exposure of
sin or exhortations about the church's future should be
brought to the leadership and left with them.

With regard to the latter kind of prophecy it is good
initially for the person who believes he is receiving
revelations from God to log a record of his prophecies
privately. In this way he can double-check when his
prophecy has been fulfilled and can be more assured that
he is not being deceived or simply carried away on an ego-
trip. This at least will give him and the leadership the
encouragement of some clear endorsement before it is
expected that prophecies of that nature should in any way
be shared with the church or acted on by the leadership. Too
many want the prophet's notoriety before they have
established a prophet's credibility. How could a church
leader take such people seriously?

A little while ago I was talking to a lady in the north of
England whom I happen to respect very much for her
commitment to the Lord. She showed me a letter she was
writing to one of our archbishops. In it she described how
she had been in York Minster one day admiring the famous
stained-glass rose window. As she did this the words 'In three

days I will destroy this temple' came vividly to her mind. She dismissed them thinking she was simply recalling relevant Scripture. But the words still kept leaping out at her. Suddenly she realised that it was not Scripture at all! What Jesus had actually said was: 'Destroy this temple, and in three days I will raise it up' (John 2:19 KJV). She was greatly puzzled. Was it in fact a lot of rubbish? It so happened that in three days the Minster was struck by fire and the window and roof, among other things, had to be renovated.

I did not think it would help the archbishop very much to get such a letter, imagining some of the many an archbishop must receive! A completely negative response would not bring her much peace of heart, especially as she felt that having been shown something so significant it must have been for some purpose.

I told her I felt that the Lord could in fact be encouraging her with a prophetic ministry and that she should note down the occasions when she felt God was speaking to her and then record what happened as a result. In this way she would be able to establish a personal history of prophecy with which she could encourage herself to step out more boldly once it was quite plain that this was in fact a gift that God had given her. I think she began to feel this might be a constructive way in which to view the whole incident.

Someone who is attempting to keep a record like this can share it in a low-key behind-the-scenes kind of way with a leader who can then be a witness to any progress, which will then be a help in the future to both. The aspiring 'prophet' should also keep a record of the times when he has got it wrong, so that he can evaluate his gift and learn to see where he may have erred. If we cannot be absolutely honest with each other it is hard to see how leader and prophet can progress very far together.

This is the sort of approach that Mike Bickle has learned through hard experience and has developed in the KCF. He also makes a point of distinguishing between people who speak prophetically — those who prophesy and those who exercise the ministry of a prophet. He deals basically with both in the same way, though not all who prophesy become prophets (and he would be very slow to recognise such an office and even slower actually to call anyone a prophet); nevertheless all prophets have to begin by prophesying.

He sees three distinct stages in the process of making prophecy edifying: the revelation itself; the interpretation of the revelation; and the application of the interpretation.

## I Revelation

I am not speaking here about how people actually receive revelations. We have seen some examples of that in the chapters on Paul Cain and Bob Jones. I am talking about the practical nature of revelations, the proper source for revelations and the possible ways of sharing them.

Revelation of itself may not always be edifying. All knowledge is not necessarily good. Its source may be deceptive. The Bible spells out carefully that there is a source of forbidden knowledge that neither man nor woman may tap. Basically, the fall of man depicted in Genesis 3 was over a desire to become wise by doing that which was forbidden:

> . . . but you must not eat from the tree of the knowledge of good and evil, for when you eat of it you will surely die. (Gen. 2:17)

> The secret things belong to the Lord our God, but the things revealed belong to us and to our children for ever . . . (Deut. 29:29)

> When the woman saw that the fruit of the tree was good for food, pleasing to the eye and desirable for gaining wisdom, she took some and ate it. She also gave some to her husband, who was with her, and he ate it. Then the eyes of both of them were opened . . . (Gen. 3:6–7)

## Anxiety of the faithful

It is perfectly natural for Bible-loving Christians to be
concerned on finding that some of their brothers in Christ
are wanting to introduce the revelatory gifts of the Spirit
into the worship and ministry of the Church. This is
especially likely to be the case where those claiming to have
the gifts are perceived as the lunatic fringe and are not in
fact well integrated with or committed to the local Body of
Christ; or when the prophet is somebody everyone knows
could easily take leave of the fellowship tomorrow, even if
slightly offended.

But there are two other reasons why such endeavours will
encounter stout opposition in the church. One is the total
unfamiliarity that many Christians have with anything of
the kind. There has been no history of exposure to such
manifestations in a wholesome environment (under authority
and in a climate where prophecy may be properly weighed
and tested), nor have most of them had any positive biblical
teaching on the subject; indeed usually the very opposite.

The other reason is that any unfamiliar experience of the
supernatural seems 'spooky'. There is genuine fear and
suspicion that anything of this nature could be an
'apparently' biblical and subtle disguise for introducing
occult influences into the worship and ministry of the
church. Evil 'New Age' teaching is already surreptitiously
insinuating itself even into the Church, just like the 'Old
Age' practices insinuated themselves into the very holy
temple of Israel (Ezek. 8). The Church can never relax her
watch. There is a constant need to be wise and vigilant.

In any situation where someone believes he has a message
from a supernatural source (a hot line from God) and
declares it to the community, there is always the possibility
that this could be counterfeit. False prophets were the bane
of Israel as they have been of the Church down the ages.
We know we must be discerning about the source of
revelation.

## Sharing revelations

We must also be very careful of the way that we use revelation. Jesus was quite specific about this and frequently explained to the disciples how he worked together with his Father. Christians who operate with revelatory gifts should bear the following four points in mind:

1  Jesus only did and said *what* he heard the Father saying and doing (John 5:19).

2  Jesus only said what the Father said and only said it *how* the Father wanted him to say it (John 12:49). There are certainly counter-productive ways of saying what we sense God is saying. Paul had this in mind, I think, when he wrote about 'speaking the truth in love' (Ephesians 4:15).

3  Jesus only said and did things *when* the Father told him, and not before (John 16:12). Even though Mary was his own mother, Jesus resisted her pressing appeal for instant intervention at the wedding in Cana of Galilee (John 2:3–4); and delayed after the urgent emotional pleas of his two friends, Martha and Mary, on the occasion of Lazarus' terminal sickness (John 11:3–6), because the time was not yet right.

4  At times, it seems, things were revealed to Jesus that he never shared (John 16:12). It is not always necessary to communicate a revelation from God. Its purpose may simply be a pointer for prayer or a guide for helping someone in need.

## Prudence is called for

Clearly any revealed knowledge must be shared with wisdom, restraint and always 'in love' — putting ourselves in the other people's shoes and sensing just how we would feel in their place. There is the temptation (arising especially if we are ambitious or insecure) to use revelation insensitively in the rush to notch up for ourselves some kind of Brownie points!

Bob Jones, a prophet of maturity, tells how the Lord showed him the impending downfall of Jimmy Swaggart which would be made public on 17 February 1988. I believe the Lord had shown this to Paul Cain some eight years previously and Paul had gone to warn Swaggart personally. Bob shared this revelation with some of his friends. Finally the day came and Bob became very excited. 'We got it — we were right on target! Jimmy Swaggart has fallen.' In the following days there was a tremendous public outcry against TV evangelists. Swaggart's name was mud. Christians were portrayed as one great bunch of hypocrites. The Lord's name was shamed.

Bob Jones tells how after a while the Lord took him on one side and rebuked him. 'That is one of my sons you were talking about — one of my sons I love has fallen and you seem pleased about it! How would you feel if people went around talking about one of your sons who had fallen from grace and caused you great shame? You should have mourned and not rejoiced.'

The Lord rebuked Bob for his spiritual pride and warned him that he would withdraw the gift from him if he misused it again. Bob was silenced and hastily withdrew to his woodshed to repent. He was very humble about it and said he wished he had had the wisdom of Paul Cain who wept before the Lord when Swaggart's final downfall had come about with all the media publicity. Bob told this story to help us avoid the pitfalls he had fallen into.

The young Joseph — that dreamer — did not share his revelations very wisely at the beginning and this aggravated his brothers, who rejected him, and embarrassed his father Jacob, who rebuked him (Gen. 37:5–11). The revelations were absolutely true and their interpretations later fulfilled on a grand scale but he lacked prudence in sharing them. It seems that the real value of the revelation was for Joseph himself, to sustain him during his hidden prison years in exile, and possibly they were never intended to be shared with anyone else anyway.

## II Interpretation

Revelations from the Lord need to be wisely handled. Often they can be quite difficult to understand. Sometimes they cannot be understood because significant events have not yet taken place. Soon after George Bush was nominated presidential candidate in 1988 by the Republican Party in the United States one of the Kansas City prophets had an enigmatic 'word' concerning him, which none of them could understand. It was a kind of riddle — one of those dark sayings the Bible talks about (Num. 12:8).

Bush was reported to be out hunting on vacation at the time. The 'word' was 'Bush is hunting quail and the quail is behind the bush!' It was not till a few weeks later that Bush nominated his choice of vice-presidential candidate — Dan Quayle — as his running mate in the forthcoming election; a nomination that came as a complete surprise to just about everyone.

This was a typical case of what seemed to be an obscure or improbable 'word' being proved in an unexpected way. So much will depend upon the interpretation and the interpretation will depend upon so much. The person who gets the revelation does not always understand the interpretation. Neither the butler nor the baker nor Pharaoh could interpret their own dreams: only Joseph was able to do that.

Before any revelation (at the level we see in the earlier chapters) is communicated to the church it is vital to share the vision first with the leadership and let them help with the interpretation.

Some people interpret out of their gifting; others interpret out of their office, just like any other ministry for the Lord — healing, for example. As there is a gift of interpretation for tongues so there is a gift for revelations which both Joseph and Daniel quite clearly had: 'Take me to the king, and I will interpret his dream for him,' said Daniel (Dan. 2:24).

Problems arise when enthusiastic Christians operating out of their own bias allow this to distort both their revelations and interpretations. In no way, however, am I saying that simply because a man has had a limited education he should be disqualified from either an authentic revelation or a valid interpretation. I think the case of Bob Jones proves that point.

At the Kansas City Fellowship they have a strict rule about bringing the prophecy to the leadership so that both prophets and pastors can consider it, provided the person submitting their prophecy comply with the following basic requirement: (Mike came up with this practice because he found that people frequently off-loaded their prophecies on him verbally while hand-shaking after the Sunday night service. He would go to bed confused and by the Monday morning was certainly none the wiser!)

Mike requests his flock to type out in full any prophecy that they wish him to receive, then to summarise the gist of it in a few lines on another clean page and to add the sender's name, phone number and the date. (Glancing at a recent but still unread letter containing some kind of prophecy hand-written across five pages of foolscap, which will take me some time to read, I find this rule a welcome one.) Having given the prophecy to the leadership the hands of the sender are now clean. The responsibility is with the leadership. They will ring if they want further elucidation.

If there are a number of independent prophecies all saying much the same thing then the leadership should pick up the drift of what God is saying easily enough when there is a real openness to the direction of the Holy Spirit.

It will not help if the sender begins to share his prophecy round and then starts counting heads to further waylay and convince the minister. He will then be less inclined to see it as a word from the Lord and more inclined to regard it as the work of a pressure group impatient of the Lord.

There is a real need for careful and prayerful interpretation. This may be seen from the following example, again from the KCF. One of the 'prophets' plainly recognised the face of a member of the fellowship in his vision. He proceeded to accuse the man he had seen of being a fraud. The man confronted flatly denied there was any truth in the accusation. Mike Bickle now began to question the 'prophet' very closely.

'I swear I saw his face and recognised this man,' said the 'prophet'.

'And what else did you see that made you think he was involved in fraud?' asked Mike.

'I saw his head in a big cloud and there were dollar signs on the cloud!' said the prophet.

Eventually it became clear that the reason the man's head was depicted as being in the clouds was because something was happening concerning him which he knew nothing about; it was all veiled from his sight. The prophet agreed that this could well be part of the interpretation. The dollar signs seemed to indicate it was to do with money. It could mean that there was some kind of financial fiddle going on somewhere which this brother needed to know about, but of which he was obviously still completely ignorant. This eventually turned out to be the case. After full investigation of the books some serious embezzlement by one of the partners in his business was uncovered. But for the very careful interpretation with the help of the pastor this might never have come to light. The great embarrassment over the confrontation gave place to thankful acknowledgment for the revelation.

Many prophets think they should be left to interpret their own revelations. Those with some experience in these things think that, generally speaking, it is best otherwise. In the multitude of counsellors there is wisdom.

## III Application

This is what we should do with the prophecy and its interpretation. Many practical questions arise here. Should the whole church be told or just a few members? Now or later? How much of the prophecy? All of it or part? Mike Bickle says that at first they shared the whole prophecy with the whole congregation – even when they still did not understand much of it. This quickly became totally unprofitable. Many of the symbols were unintelligible and the parables and enigmas insoluble. The bottom line in the operation of the gifts must be the common good (1 Cor. 12:7). Sharing the whole prophecy to the whole congregation was clearly not ministering to the common good in their situation. In fact, it soon became very counter-productive and aroused hostility towards any kind of prophecy.

They now rarely tell the whole congregation anything until there is a reason to do so – that is, when the Lord has clearly led them to take some action for the common good that the congregation needs to know about.

For instance, when Noel Alexander joined the staff they were able to share with the church how the Lord had led them to take him on, starting with Bob's strange word to Mike at one of the prayer meetings when he blurted out, 'The Lord says Noel is coming!' Had they shared that with the congregation initially it would doubtless have left everyone both bemused and confused.

Most revelation of this kind is simply to confirm some individual's personal direction by God or to enlighten someone in his personal intercessions for others. Many of the prophecies given to the leaders were meant for the leaders personally. This was John Wimber's testimony regarding the immense help he was given from Paul Cain living in mid-America, Dallas, during a 1988 leadership crisis at Anaheim on the West Coast.

Prophets may be led to share other prophecies with other individual members in the congregation privately, provided the leadership does not object, and this was the case in the story we have already told about Bob Jones, who went up to Art Katz and revealed things which led to blessing on a much wider front and eventually included Mike Bickle himself.

# 11

## Restoring the Prophetic Ministry to the Church

A small conference on prophecy was advertised for the end
of April 1987. It was to be held in Birmingham, Alabama.
Mike Bickle was booked as the main speaker. Several of the
prophets from Kansas City went along with him. One of
those attending was Paul Cain, someone we know Mike had
long wanted to meet. Whether those from Kansas City knew
that Paul Cain would be present is not clear but Paul
certainly knew that Mike Bickle would be there as his name
had been advertised on the programme. At one stage during
the conference the host suggested to Mike that it might seem
appropriate to invite Paul to say a few words to the rest of
the conference, whereupon Paul came forward to prophesy.
His words were all directed towards the Kansas City team.
What they heard astounded them.

Everything that their local prophets had already been
sharing among themselves about revival breaking out in
Kansas City and spreading to the far corners of the earth
was being confirmed to them in this almost incredible way.
It had to be God! They just knew it. By the end of the
prophecy the whole party from Kansas City was on the floor
weeping before the Lord.

After the meeting was over they introduced themselves
to Paul Cain, initiating a warm friendship which has since
flourished. It was only natural that they should invite him
to Kansas City and Paul visited them within the fortnight,
on 10–12 May.

## A dark saying

Prior to his visit the KCF had been seeking and praying about a new centre for worship, as their old meeting hall, which seated 700, was no longer big enough. One of the prophets had been given a vision of the new place and the detail which impressed everyone was that there appeared to be a lot of green grass involved with it; the prophet said he definitely saw green grass!

This was quite obviously another of those 'dark sayings' that God sometimes gives his people to puzzle and pray over. Some thought it implied that the building would be on a street with a name that could naturally be associated with 'green grass' – perhaps 'Grassways' or 'Meadow Lane'! Others felt it must have something to do with a new building on ground that at the moment was still grassed over! It really was a teaser and they had a lot of fun trying to 'suss' it all out.

One day Mike had a visit from a couple of Christian businessmen who owned a sports complex in Grandview Road that was not going very well. They wanted to sell up. They had felt that if there was any Christian concern that was interested they would be willing to sell cheaply and so help the Lord's work.

They suggested to Mike that he should take a look at it. Before doing this he needed to verify that the place could actually hold 5000 people. Mike was remembering other prophecies with regard to that number. He also checked that there was permission from the fire officers and so on for seating so many.

He then took some of his leadership team round to see the place. As soon as they got there they knew that these must be the premises God had planned for them. The floor was covered with a carpet of artificial grass – a surface required for the athletics and the ball games which had been held there. The deal was negotiated quickly and they were soon in. The green grass flooring is still there, not only looking fresh and pleasant but as a constant reminder of God's wonderful leading and provision.

## Joel's army training centre

By the time Paul Cain arrived in Kansas City the fellowship was well settled into their new meeting place at their Grandview Worship Centre. Paul immediately recognised the locality from the crossroads outside as the place which the Lord had showed him many times (possibly twenty, over as many years) as a spiritual training centre for the soldiers of Joel's army that God was raising up for the coming revival.

'Many years ago,' said Paul, 'I came to the crossroads of life and I saw a vision of an illuminated bill-board on which was written: "Joel's army in training" and it was on these crossroads with an arrow pointing to this spot — though there was no building on it then! I believe God has shown me that here he is going to raise up an army. This army is not a destructive army but a deliverance army. God is not going to work in a major way through superstar Christians any more, but through ordinary soldiers who will hear God's Spirit in the midst of this Laodicean age which is rampaging the Church. These soldiers will be genuine "Jesus" people. They will need to strip themselves for service. There is no Mickey-Mouse religion for them.

'The Lord is raising up a new breed of Christians who will not be looking for their own glory. A new breed of leaders and teachers is coming — Joel's army — who will be working for the glory of God. Many years ago the American Indians used to go through the forests in single file. Each Indian would put his moccasin in the step of the man in front of him. The enemy would see the footprint and say an Indian had passed that way. They never realised it was a large fighting force. In the days to come, when the blind see, the deaf hear and the lame walk, the people will no longer say, "Kathryn Kuhlman passed this way today" or "Reinhardt Bonnke passed this way today". No, they will say "Jesus passed this way today!" There will be no other footprints, only the footprints of Jesus who alone will have all the glory.'

Although Paul had actually seen a vision of this spot many times he was fearful about visiting it in case he found men and women there of the wrong spirit. When he heard Mike Bickle's message about new wineskins in preparation for the coming revival his heart was warmed. When he recognised the seriousness of God's calling upon them, the simplicity of their lifestyles, their discipline in fasting and intercession, their yearning after holiness and their care for the poor he was deeply moved. It was an exciting confirmation for Paul to discover at last the actual place he had seen so often in his vision, and also for Mike to have the added assurance of God's purposes for the Kansas City Fellowship; Mike and the leadership certainly and sincerely wanted Jesus to have all the glory.

Those two days with Paul Cain were mutually beneficial in other ways also. There was great blessing through Paul Cain's public ministry to the fellowship. But the discovery of the Kansas City Fellowship was a blessing to Paul Cain as well.

## Ministry to leaders

We have already referred to Paul's health. He was obviously not well and his heart was playing up considerably. This may have been partly attributable to the particular kind of stressful ministry he had had. Every now and then Paul was led by God to seek out a leader privately, be he a spiritual one, an industrialist or a politician. Often the revelations were so stunning and the warnings so serious that the recipients would become quite offensive. Sometimes, like the woman of Samaria who said, 'Come, see a man who told me everything I ever did' (John 4:29) – a slight exaggeration to say the least – the recipients would mistakenly assume that because Paul had been shown some things very clearly he must therefore know everything!

Like many other prophets before him Paul Cain has had threats upon his life because of this. He has never altogether shaken off the possibility that he might one day meet a grizzly end at the hands of the Mafia or some other mercenary. Not a pleasant prospect! Who would be a prophet?

It is easy to see how this lonely kind of ministry can take its toll and Paul was increasingly concerned about the lack of intercessory prayer backing he would have once his aged mother passed on; she was over 104 and could not live for ever. He was very dependent upon her for her committed spiritual support. Where could he ever hope to get such sympathetic and understanding coverage as that which she provided for him through her intercessions and communion with the Lord? Wherever would he look for the kind of wise and godly counsel she had given him all his life?

An answer to all this was slowly becoming plain to Mike Bickle. After praying it over he felt led to invite Paul to come up from Dallas and join the team in Kansas City, should anything happen to his mother. This Paul has felt right to accept — indeed he is profoundly grateful. And members of the Kansas City Fellowship are already committed to interceding for Paul. Those who know him say that his health has already improved markedly and his ministry increased powerfully.

There is even a project afoot there, in response to prophecy, to set up a kind of sanctuary near Kansas City for five or six members of the prophetic team and their families. It will be called Shiloh. Since it is expected that the team will be increasingly involved in travel it is intended that it will become a shelter for restoration of their physical health, spiritual vitality and emotional well-being, and protect them from the urgency and demands of their ministries. It will definitely not be a 'visitors' centre'.

## Paul Cain and John Wimber meet

In 1988 Paul Cain sensed the Lord telling him to go and see John Wimber in California. An intermediary for Paul in Dallas, Jack Deere, phoned and asked for an appointment. Though extremely grateful for his help at a critical time earlier in the year, John was under pressure and was not too keen on the idea of meeting Paul. Jack urged John to make a special effort since Paul felt such a meeting was very important for both of them. Paul would accept any time that was convenient.

Eventually John was able to dig out five dates to offer him in the autumn. Jack Deere thanked him and said Paul would book the second one. 'By the way,' he added, 'so that you will know that God has a strategic purpose in this for Paul and the Vineyard movement, Paul says there will be an earthquake that day!'

Jack asked Paul if it was going to be a big earthquake. Paul had replied, 'No, but a big earthquake will occur on the day I leave.'

As John Wimber commented when we were over there later, 'To predict an earthquake for southern California is no big deal – we do get them here – but to predict the exact date for an earthquake so far ahead has to be significant.'

And there was an earthquake in California as Paul had predicted on the very day he arrived! Paul did not say where the earthquake would be on the day he left California; but there was in fact a terrible one on 7 December 1988, the day he left. It was in Armenia and was reported worldwide.

It had not been easy for Paul to leave Dallas for California either. The night before he left, evil materialised in his room in the form of a young man who told him that if he went to California he would kill him! But after praying all night Paul set off in faith.

When Paul finally met John Wimber he was surprised. For a couple of years he had been searching for the Christian

leader God had told him about who would give him a
platform to use for the restoration of the prophetic ministry
to the church. Somehow he had never imagined that John
Wimber could be that man. John was too busy with the
vision God had given him and would be in too much demand
to cope with Paul's vision and particular call from God —
so Paul Cain seems to have rationalised.

Now that they had met, Paul was able to minister to John*
all that God had laid on his heart for him. Paul was greatly
moved at the open and humble way John received him.
Then, quite clearly, the Lord told Paul that this was the man
he had been raising up to help Paul restore the prophetic
ministry to the church.

## Complaining to John Wimber

Mary and I had flown on to California to stay a couple of
days to meet John and Carol Wimber, at their kind
invitation. This was about five months after their own link-
up with Paul and we had not had a chance to discuss it.
There was so much to talk to them about after our mind-
blowing weekend in Kansas City. It was good to be able to
relax with friends. We certainly had some thoughts to
ventilate to them — especially as John had been the one who
originally introduced this level of prophetic ministry to us
through Mike Bickle. Then there was a possibility that John
might one day introduce Paul Cain to Britain.

'How could one really ever sponsor that kind of thing?'
I asked John.

We mentioned Paul's style of preaching which had
concerned us. Probably, I think, what worried us most was
the reaction our evangelical friends in England would have
should they ever hear Paul preach.

I said, 'Do you know that when he got up to preach that
evening he announced a verse which he said the Lord had

* See Wimber's account of the effect of that visit upon him in his publication
*Equipping the Saints*, Fall 1989.

impressed upon him some seven different ways. I thought
to myself that this must be going to be a good sermon; he's
really got a burden for it! He gave us the biblical reference
for the verse but then he never read it out or preached from
it! Would you believe it?' I shook my head sadly at the
memory of such a let-down!

John glanced towards me. 'Did you look it up?'

'No!' I said, 'it never occurred to me to do that because
he went on to preach about something else!'

'Well, I imagine that was what you were meant to do,'
said John simply.

'Of course,' I thought, 'what a fool I have been. Why
did I never think of looking it up?'

I thought I had better be careful about airing my other
doubts too readily after that. I did not mention my problem
with Paul's obvious Pentecostal theology. It all seemed much
less serious as we considered that when God puts his
treasures in earthen vessels these vessels will reflect their own
earthly views: be they cultural, theological, psychological,
emotional, ecclesiastical or social. Prophets are only human.
No matter how impressive the prophet he still only 'sees in
part' and what we need to glean from him is the purest
reflection of his original revelation and then weigh it, sift
it, interpret it and apply it.

But that was not all that I did not share at that time.
Another thing that had stuck in my evangelical gullet was
a comment made by Paul when he quoted a certain verse
of the Bible and said that the King James Version gave the
best interpretation of what God really meant concerning that
text! 'How could a man who was obviously not a linguist,'
I argued with myself, 'say what a text actually meant?'

Even as I was cogitating over this, another question arose
within me by way of an answer. Was it not within the realms
of possibility that a man who prayed and meditated so long
and conscientiously over the Word of God, and received
such clear revelations from the Lord about present-day

situations, could be shown what the Spirit of God really intended when the original 'God-breathed' word was written (2 Tim. 3:16).

And we could just as easily turn the question round: 'How could a linguist who might not have the disciplined devotional life of a man like Paul Cain and had never experienced anything like the revelations that Paul had done, necessarily claim to have a better understanding of what God really meant in certain debatable passages?' Obviously no prophet could dilute or distort Scripture or twist it to mean something that was incompatible with the text or context, or contrary to the plain teaching of the rest of Scripture — indeed the prophet himself must subject all his own insights and revelations to the Word of God for testing. But a prophet might sometimes have better insights than the experts! Prophecy and teaching are distinctive ministries to help get the balance right.

There seemed no doubt that the prophets we had met were humble, kindly, generous, godly and dedicated men and women of prayer. They deferred to Mike Bickle their leader and to one another in a truly beautiful way. They really loved the Lord and studied his Word. Though we had left them with so many questions still on our lips, and with yet more that were still to surface, we had to admit that we really liked these people and they were good to be with. One felt oneself thirsting after righteousness, living and worshipping among them. We had to admit that it certainly seemed that they were receiving prophecies at a high level of revelation and these were being confirmed with remarkable signs.

We had certainly never met anything like this before, and that was in spite of many years working in Chile where we had observed Pentecostalism at first hand. We had met many strange things there, such as people, even in our own churches, having their teeth miraculously filled (*creatio ex nihilo*), but we had never come across anything quite like this high level of prophecy out there.

Every now and again we heard of prophecies being fulfilled to the letter but they were usually 'one-offs'. A lady once foretold a major earthquake in central Chile in May 1960, but to the best of our knowledge she did not have a prophetic ministry that was verifiably sustained over a prolonged period. Indeed, we certainly had no idea that it was possible to find such a prophetic ministry being exercised in a Christian church anywhere in the world today, though there seems no obvious reason from the Bible why this should not be the case.

## A paradigm shift

We felt we were experiencing a paradigm shift — beginning to see another way of looking at the foundational things we held dear, without having in any way to discard them. Perhaps that is what the Bible meant when it spoke about scales falling from Paul's eyes. He was experiencing a paradigm shift in that street called Straight! Some professed Christians have discarded the Bible on the grounds that they could not believe the Lord had revealed himself throughout history in the ways the biblical writers depicted. We have never had any real problem with that.

But what about revelations today? And why now after all these centuries? And so late in one's ministry! And why was it Americans who seemed to have the 'hot-lines' to God? John and Carol doubtless had their own answers to similar questions and others, but when we were through they turned to look at each other in obvious amusement and laughed. They felt they had just listened to a complete replay from our lips of their own objections, which they too had struggled over.

It was by no means the first time in their ministry that they had encountered a dilemma of this kind. They could not forget the first time in 1980 when the Spirit of God had fallen with great and unaccustomed power upon the Vineyard they were pastoring in Orange Country,

California. Not knowing what to make of all the associated phenomenology, John had stayed up all night searching the Scriptures, praying, and looking up the history of revivals. Very early the next morning, still uncertain what to make of it all, he had had a long-distance phone call from a friend in Denver, who said that God had given him a message for John when he was praying for him early that morning. He could not understand what it meant, he said. It was simply God saying something like, 'It's all right, John. That was ME!' How often since then have I heard John himself say, 'Why can't we just let God be God.' Sometimes it can be very difficult but sooner or later we have to adjust to the fact that he is sovereign and can do what he likes, how he likes and when he likes.

## What should we think?

So how do we conclude? Is there going to be a restoration of the prophetic ministry to the Church? Are we going to see revival on a grand scale? Will there be persecutions? Are we really living in the end times?

I have to say that, in spite of the tragic claims down the ages of some who have sincerely, but mistakenly, believed themselves to be prophets, I do not see any problem in believing that, from a biblical perspective, this could be a very genuine prophetic ministry which, in accordance with God's will, is being restored to the Church today. After all, Paul deals succinctly with the gift of prophecy in 1 Corinthians 14:3, clearly seeing it as a gift for the Church. He also reminds the readers in his Ephesians letter (4:8–11) that Jesus, *after his ascension*, gave gifts to men. Among those post-ascension gifts there was prophecy. Prophets may have been frustrated and persecuted but the gift should never 'again be denied nor prophecy forbidden its proper place in the ordered life of the Church. This is not to say that prophets of this kind are meant to take up much time at gatherings for public worship for reasons already explained elsewhere.

Prophecy of this revelatory kind does not have to be regarded as a pre-Christian thing. But too many 'prophets' have simply pretended to have the gift or used it counter-productively and there is little credibility for such 'prophets' today. Also too often critics have behaved badly towards the prophet – considering the superficial directives recommended in the early days of the primitive Church in the *Didache* – down to the discounting of all such revelatory prophecy today or the branding of all prophecy as occult. These latter negative approaches are very crushing to anyone just beginning to receive revelations from God. The holy gift is threatened with strangulation at birth.

The kind of prophecy we have mentioned in this book is not in fact quite such an affront to the intellect because it is delivered with the promise of accompanying signs, the fulfilment of which enhances credibility.

## Persecution and the 'end time' overtones

When the early Church began to be persecuted (Acts 5) the disciples were soon dispersed abroad. As this happened the Church grew. This constituted a threat to the State and the persecution consequently spread and intensified. There is no reason to believe we should be spared persecution if revival comes again on the grand scale foretold by the Old Testament prophets. Indeed, the New Testament endorses this view (see Matthew 24:9–14 and Revelation 13:14–17 etc).

Finally, the 'latter days' element of these prophecies needs to be looked at fairly and squarely since this has been one of the common features in so many of the false prophecies down the ages. (Some examples of this were spelt out in chapter one.) But in this case, though there have been prophecies about the last days and the Laodicean age for the Church, no dates have ever been set for the Lord's return by these Kansas City prophets, nor would we believe they would ever do anything so foolish. They are far too well grounded in Scripture to be so deceived. We cannot discount them for seeing their prophecies in terms of 'the last days' because it is possible that these are indeed the end times.

In one sense we have been living in the last days ever since God finally spoke to us through his Son (Heb. 1:2), but there have to be days which are imminent to those days before the Lord's eventual second coming. We could well be living in those lawless days now.

The prophecy of Joel was wisely quoted by Peter in Acts 2 as relevant, but it is obvious that Pentecost was only a partial fulfilment of Joel 2:28. It still awaits the last days when the Spirit will come in some fresh and final way, and our sons and daughters will prophesy.

We are almost on the threshold of a new millennium — the year 2000 whose coming will provide a major 'time mark' in history, and an obvious impetus for preachers of all kinds to focus on the end times; yet these days in which we live may still prove to be the last days. No one can possibly demonstrate that these prophets are wrong to talk in this way because only the future can reveal who is right in this matter. There are good grounds, as we have seen, for thinking that these prophets are being faithful to the Lord in speaking out as they do. They sincerely believe God is showing them things that are to happen in the last days. They give signs quite beyond man's ability to manipulate as back-up for their predictions. Plenty of people have been wrong about this before and have made fools of themselves by fixing dates in plain contradiction of Scripture. Even as I wrote this, a group of fundamentalist Christians were expecting the Rapture to happen that very same week! How wrong they were!

### Someone must be right someday

Sooner or later someone will have to be right about the proximity of the last days though he would never be right to predict actual dates (Acts 1:7). The last days are certainly coming. Jesus himself taught about them (Matt. 24) in terms of the conclusion of the age. This age itself is the last temporal era (Heb. 1:2). The last days of the last age could be here soon but, before they come, Jesus said that 'this gospel of the kingdom will be preached in the whole world as a testimony to all nations, and then the end will come' (Matt. 24:14). The end of the era will not come before every nation has heard the Good News and then Christ will come again. That's how the Church has always understood it! That is how we must understand it now and that is how it will surely be!

Since beginning to write this book, reports have appeared in both the religious and secular press (see *Christian Newsworld*, December 1989, and the *Evening Standard* [London] 25 November 1989) that the astronaut James Erwin has flown by helicopter over a particular site on the borders of Turkey with Armenia and claimed that the remains of the Ark have been located. We await fuller reports. Revival too is reported to have broken out in Armenia recently. This was also part of Bob Jones's prophecy connected with the finding of Noah's Ark mentioned in the introduction to this book.

Now we await news of Pat, Mike Bickle's brother, who is a paraplegic. Should he get healed . . . then . . . watch this space! That would be amazing! Surely it would constitute the most encouraging sign that the other predictions which have come out of Kansas, the Prophetic City, concerning revival are about to be fulfilled. Furthermore it would seem that the promises about the restoration of the prophetic office through the Church (the corporate Elijah) will become a renewed spiritual reality in evangelism to prepare the world for the glorious second coming of Christ and the awesome Day of Judgment.

# Appendix

## Forbidden Communications

### Scripture examined

We need to examine Scripture to see which sources man is permitted to communicate with and which not. The Bible is emphatically opposed to man's attempting any communication with the occult (including the dead).

To simplify our understanding of this, there are two particular Hebrew words we need to know, *Ob* and *Yiddeoni*. Following J. Stafford Wright (see below), we take the liberty of forming the plurals for these two unfamiliar Hebrew words by simply adding an 's'.

1  *Ob* – the 'O' is long and the 'b' is pronounced almost like a 'v'. The King James Authorised Version always translates this word as 'familiar spirit' but it can also imply the medium (Lev. 20:27) who is communicating with this familiar or controlling spirit. The precise meaning of *Ob* is uncertain, but a similar word in Arabic means 'to return'.

2  *Yiddeoni* – the final 'o' and 'i' are long. In the King James Authorised Version this is always translated as wizard. *Yiddeoni* is connected with the Hebrew word 'to know'.

### Communicating spirits

Both words appear to involve a communicating spirit. The main references are:

Do not turn to *obs* (mediums) or seek out *yiddeonis* (spiritists) for you will be defiled by them. I am the Lord your God. (Lev. 19:31)

I will set my face [says the Lord] against the person who turns to *obs* (mediums) and *yiddeonis* (spiritists) to prostitute himself by following them, and I will cut him off from his people. (Lev. 20:6)

A man or woman who is an *ob* (medium) or *yiddeoni* (spiritist) among you must be put to death. (Lev. 20:27; cf. also Exod. 22:18)

Let no-one be found among you . . . who is an *ob* (medium) or *yiddeoni* (spiritist) or who consults the dead (necromancer). (Deut. 18:10−11. This is part of a more comprehensive list of occult practices to be found among the Canaanite inhabitants who were being driven out of the Promised Land.)

The nations you will dispossess listen to those who practise sorcery or divination. But as for you, the Lord your God has not permitted you to do so. (Deut. 18:14)

## Backsliding monarchs

Saul had expelled the *obs* (mediums) and the *yiddeonis* (spiritists) from the land (1 Sam. 28:3). Then in his rebellion from God and subsequent desolation he sought out an *ob* (medium).

'Find me a woman who is an *ob* (medium) so that I may go and enquire of her' (1 Sam. 28:7).

They replied, 'There is one (an *ob*) in Endor.'

Saul ordered the woman to 'Consult an *ob* (controlling spirit) . . . and bring up for me the one I name' (1 Sam. 28:8).

This was his crowning act of rebellion against God.

'Saul died because he was unfaithful to the Lord; he did not keep the word of the Lord, and even consulted an *ob* (medium) for guidance, and did not enquire of the Lord. So the Lord put him to death' (1 Chron. 10:13–14).

Saul was not the only king who led God's people astray. Among the list of King Manasseh's sins it is recorded that he used *obs* and *yiddeonis* (2 Kgs 21:6; 2 Chron. 33:6).

## Reforms promoted

The reforming king Josiah 'got rid of the *obs* (mediums) and *yiddeonis* (spiritists)' (2 Kgs. 23:24).

Isaiah is relentless in driving home God's law on this detestable practice: 'When men tell you to consult *obs* (mediums) and *yiddeonis* (spiritists) who whisper (high pitch) and mutter (low pitch), should not a people enquire of their God? Why consult the dead on behalf of the living? To the law and to the testimony!' (Isa. 8:19–20).

## Spiritist mediums

In *Christianity and the Occult* (from which source I have drawn heavily) J. Stafford Wright, a leading Old Testament scholar of his day, suggests that since in the Bible the word *ob* is sometimes used by itself, whereas *yiddeoni* is always linked with an *ob*, it would be reasonable to suppose that the *ob* is the main control spirit and the *yiddeonis* are the spirits called up by the control spirit *ob*.

The Hebrew, however, does not only imply that an *ob* is a control spirit, but that it may also be a man or a woman (Lev. 20:27). A person who has a controlling spirit becomes a control spirit – a medium. Most modern-day mediums appear to have one or two controlling spirits in tow. Mediums open themselves up to being channels for communication with the spirits of darkness. The punishment for mediums in the Old Testament was death.

Although the New Testament does modify some of the social and food regulations of the Old Testament, it never withdraws the ban on contact with spirits. On the positive side the New Testament encourages Christians to build up a relationship with God the Father through Jesus Christ.

The spirits of darkness (demons) are unclean and it is noticeable that those who communicate with them very quickly get led into acts of impurity and will soon lead others into the ways of uncleanness. The Holy Spirit of God is purity and light and enjoins the followers of Jesus Christ to be holy and to walk in the light.

It is then a perfectly proper concern for the Church today to be wary lest in any desire to be open to revelations from God we overlook the clear warnings given concerning all the pagan practices plainly forbidden in the Bible.

## Detestable practices

We have been at pains positively to encourage the operation of the proper revelatory gifts of the Spirit which are holy and supernatural in origin, but there is a basic list of abominable pagan practices which is derived from the occult, a satanic counterfeit of God's true supernatural power.

This manifests itself in three areas: miracles, communication and knowledge of the future.

Such practice is forbidden because:

- It places a person under the control of a power which is not God's — a power which is hostile to the Lord. (1 Cor. 10:19–21)
- The lust for certain knowledge which was forbidden to mankind was the cause of man's fall — it is portrayed as an attempt to by-pass God's specifically stated boundaries. (Gen. 3:3–5)
- The desire for such power to spiritually dominate and control others is opposed to God's will. (Exod. 3:7–9; Isa. 47:12–15; Micah 6:8)
- It creates a dangerous and destructive personality. (Mark 3:27; 5:1–20)
- It is rank disobedience to God; this is rebellion and arrogance. (1 Sam. 15:23)

- This road tends to lead downhill into increasingly unclean, degenerating and destructive practices.

## Solemn warnings

Solemn warnings were repeatedly given to God's chosen people who were about to enter the Promised Land (Deut. 19:9—13). They were to beware the forbidden practices employed by the Canaanite inhabitants, who were being driven out precisely because of such abominations. The list is spelt out as follows:

1  Februation. This is the terribly cruel practice of passing offspring of either sex through fire (as sacrifices to heathen gods [Deut. 12:31] ), supposedly to placate a pagan deity for obtaining some favour or averting some calamity.

2  Divination. This was the most prevalent of occult activities in ancient heathendom. It has reappeared in every epoch of human history. In nearly every part of the world evangelised by pioneer Christian missionaries there has been opposition from heathen practitioners of divination. The following list will help to identify some techniques for divination though there are many more: arithmancy (from numbers); coffee-grout reading; bird formation in flight; horoscopy (star-reading); geomancy (dot-reading); cartomancy (card-reading); crystal glass gazing; capromancy (smoke-reading); pyromancy (fire-reading); tephromancy (ash-reading); tealeaf-reading in cups; radaesthenia; pendulums; white-of-egg reading in wine-glasses.

3  Sorcery. The securing of a desired answer by tampering or introducing secret influences (magic) to operate in one's favour.

4  Soothsaying. This is especially linked with divination. Both are arts for the unlawful acquisition of

knowledge of the future. There is an alternative translation for Numbers 23:23, which is very pertinent. It runs: 'There is no omen in Jacob and no divination in Israel. At the appropriate time in Jacob and Israel God gives the revelation.' *Whenever it is the right time God will speak to his people by the prophets*. The verse makes a clear distinction between the illegitimate acquisition of knowledge from the powers of darkness and the legitimate means for obtaining information from God.

5 The practice of witchcraft. Something which is on the increase again in the Western world today.

6 Spell-casting – which effected what amounted to curses. Ezekiel refers to certain women who made use of magic wrist-bands and veils to put death curses on people and to give assurance of personal safety to others (Ezek. 13:17–23).

7 Mediumistic practices with a control spirit (already referred to).

8 Spiritism (already referred to).

9 Necromancy – consulting the dead – a comprehensive term which includes all forms of spiritism and superstition.

## Immorality and idolatry

These detestable practices (they were associated with gross immorality [Lev. 20] and idolatry [Lev. 26[ ) were a constant temptation to the people of Israel when they fell into backsliding and only served to prove that the warnings were indeed all too necessary.

Manasseh, King of Judah, is on record as leading Israel into doing more evil than all the nations who had been driven out by the Lord (see 2 Kgs 21:6,9).

## The sentence of death

The Old Testament solemnly pronounces the death penalty

upon those who fall into such heathen rites (Exod. 22:18; Lev. 20:6, 20, 27; Deut. 17:5). Any Christian believer today who seeks to be open to revelations of the Spirit from the Lord God Almighty must certainly renounce every such practice which can only lead to defilement, abomination and ultimate destruction for himself and all who follow him.

# References

Henry Chadwick, *The Early Church*. Penguin, 1968.

Rex Gardner, *Healing Miracles*. Darton, Longman & Todd, 1986.

Wayne Grudem, *The Gift Of Prophecy*. Kingsway, 1988

D. E. Harrell, *All Things are Possible*. Indiana University Press, 1975.

Walter J. Hollenweger, *The Pentecostals*. Augsburg Fortress, 1977.

F. J. A. Hort, *The Ante-Nicene Fathers*. 1895. W. B. Eerdmans, 1951.

Kurt Koch, *Christian Counselling and Occultism*. Kregel Publications, Grand Rapids, 1972.

Ronald A. Knox, *Enthusiasm*. N. E. Collins, 1987.

Christian Lalive d'Epinay, *Haven of the Masses*. Lutterworth Press, 1969.

Howard Pittman, *Placebo*. Published privately by the author (before November 1983).

John Pridmore, '*Miracles: the Mystery and the Meaning*'. *Crusade* magazine, October 1976.

*Grace City Report*, Special Edition, Volume 2, Number 5. Kansas City, August 1989.

John and Paula Sandford, *The Elijah Task*. Logos International, Plainfields, 1977.

Keith Thomas, *Religion and the Decline of Magic*. Penguin, 1973.

John Wimber, *Equipping the Saints*. Vineyard Ministries International, Fall 1989.

J. Stafford Wright, *Christianity and the Occult*. Scripture Union, London, 1971.